EVERYTHING
ONEDRIVE

A-Z Mastery Guide for Exploring Microsoft OneDrive for File Storage, Sharing & Syncing + Professional Hacks, Tips & Tricks for File Management

CARTY BINN

CONTENTS

INTRODUCTION

If you want to learn how to utilize Microsoft OneDrive, you've come to the best place. In this book, you'll learn how to use Microsoft OneDrive to save, share, and sync your files. It offers you a thorough knowledge of how to use Microsoft OneDrive if it's new to you and you're just getting started, and by the end of this book, you'll be able to use OneDrive like a Pro. Also, there are some great tips for you towards the end of the book.

Microsoft OneDrive is one of the world's most popular Cloud Storage services. It allows you to save all of your important files and documents, even encrypted ones. You can access them at any time and from any location, or you can share them with a colleague or partner. Even better, OneDrive integrates seamlessly with all Microsoft Suite productivity programs, including Word, Excel, PowerPoint, and others. This book will walk you through the process of using OneDrive.

CHAPTER 1

UNDERSTANDING ONEDRIVE

Welcome to the first chapter. You'll get a fast overview of what Microsoft OneDrive is, what the Cloud is, how to back up your data to the cloud, and how to access and use Microsoft OneDrive on your computer, the web, and your phone.

What exactly is OneDrive?

OneDrive is primarily an online storage service (you get up to 5 GB of storage for free). It is a document collaboration tool, allowing you to share and collaborate on the same document with others. It is also a backup application that enables you to save your documents to the cloud so that you have more than one copy in case your desktop or laptop is damaged. OneDrive can also be used as a free Microsoft office tool, allowing you to create, edit, delete, and otherwise manipulate Microsoft Office documents. This implies that you can generate and modify Microsoft Office files without having to pay a licensing cost. OneDrive is a productivity tool as well; it enables you to organize your files for simple access and search, and you can access them from any device, including laptops, desktops, and mobile devices.

It is, after all, a Cloud Storage service provider. It's the same thing as iCloud or Google Drive, only it's Microsoft's version. What exactly does it mean to keep your data in the cloud? We all know that clouds float above us, but what does it mean to place a file in one of them? The simplest way to think about it is that you have your computer at home, and when you put a file or a document in the Cloud, you're putting it on Microsoft's computer. Microsoft refers to their computers as Servers, and their servers are located in various data centers around the world, but whenever you put a file in the Cloud, it's on one of these servers in these data centers.

Why Should You Use OneDrive?

You may be wondering why you would ever want to do that and what the advantages of storing your information in the Cloud are. There are three major advantages to storing your files in the Cloud:

Backup your files

You can make a backup of your data. Say you have a lot of data on your laptop, and if you lose your laptop, it is stolen, or your hard drive fails, by backing up your information in the Cloud, your contents are secure; you can then restore all of your files.

Access your files from any location

Another advantage is that you can access your files from any location. For example, if you reside in Seattle and have all of your data on your computer here in Seattle, and you go on a vacation to Europe and want to access your files, it will be difficult since your computer is at home. Instead, you simply access the Cloud, which contains all of your files, and then access them from anywhere.

Share and collaborate

The third advantage is that you can share and collaborate on your documents with others. What exactly do we mean by that? When you work on a file on your computer and want to share it with someone, you would normally email it to them, they would make some modifications, and then you would send it back. By keeping a file in the Cloud, you can share a link to that file and continue working on that file through that link, and anybody you share it with can also work on that file, eliminating the need to transfer files back and forth. It greatly simplifies cooperation.

Installing OneDrive

Installing on Your Desktop PC or Mac

We are going to look at how you can get OneDrive, so if these things interest you and you are interested in utilizing the Cloud and OneDrive, let's go on the computer and look at how you can get started here.

You have just logged into your personal computer. If you are using Windows 10, getting started with OneDrive is simple since it is already pre-installed on Windows 10. This means that you do not need to do any further steps to get OneDrive; you can immediately begin making use of it. If you are using an earlier version of Windows, such as Windows 7 or Windows 8, you may still upgrade to Windows 10, and if you do so, OneDrive will be made available to you without any further action required on your part. You can still download and install OneDrive on your computer even if you are using Windows 7 or 8 and you do not want to update to Windows 10.

The first thing that you need to do is visit the website

www.microsoft.com/en-us/microsoft-365/OneDrive/download. This is the required starting point.

Not only can you download and install OneDrive on Windows 7 or Windows 8, but you can also install it on a Mac. This means that it does not matter what operating system you are currently using since you will still be able to acquire OneDrive.

Installing On iOS and Android devices

Next, let's have a look at the process that will enable you to use Microsoft OneDrive on your mobile device; regardless of whether you have an iPhone or an Android phone, you can download and install OneDrive. If you are using an iPhone, go to the App Store to download the OneDrive app; if you are using an Android device, go to the Play Store to get the app.

When you have entered the App Store or the Play Store, click the icon that looks like a magnifying glass and type **"OneDrive"** into the search bar. When you search OneDrive, you should see that the top result is labeled **"Microsoft OneDrive."** If you already have it installed, all you need to do is click on "**Open**." If you haven't yet installed it, go ahead and click on "**Install**," and then you'll have OneDrive on your phone as well.

You will be able to access your files from your desktop computer, as well as from any other computer, and even from your phone when you are on the go if you also install OneDrive on your phone. This means that you will genuinely have access to your files from everywhere.

Let's go back to the computer so you can see how to get started with OneDrive on your computer. You have successfully installed OneDrive on your personal computer; now the question is, how do you get started utilizing OneDrive, and what should you do next?

Pricing

How do you obtain OneDrive if you are interested in acquiring it and how much space do you get with OneDrive if you think that OneDrive seems quite compelling? If you sign up for a free OneDrive account over on the right-hand side, you will get 5 GB of storage space free of charge, and that is about all there is to it.

Any file, anywhere, always protected

There are certain circumstances in which **5 GB** of storage will not be sufficient; hence, if you just need a little bit more space, you can pay for it, and for an additional two dollars per month, you can have **100 GB** of storage. Although **100 GB** is often a decent place to begin, OneDrive does have the option to purchase more space beyond that amount if you so choose. If you do so, you can expand your storage to more than **100 GB**. On the left-hand side of the page are two different plans, and this is the Microsoft 365 plan: they have a **Personal plan**, which is designed for one person, and you have a **Family plan**, which you can use with up to six people at a time. You will get **1 TB** of storage space with the personal plan for about **70 dollars**, and 6 **TB** of storage space with the Family plan for about **100 dollars**. This is probably more storage space than you'll ever need, so even if you have a lot of videos, you're still well under the **1 TB** limit.

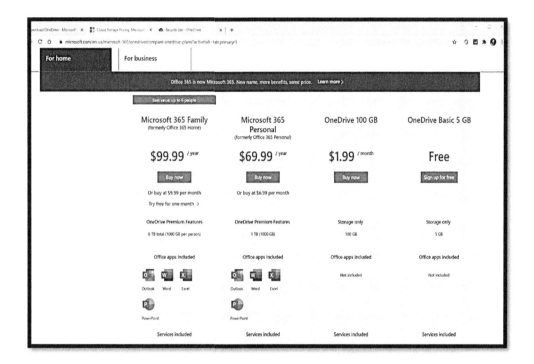

Not only do you receive storage space on the Cloud, but you also get the different Office applications such as Outlook, Word, Excel, and PowerPoint. This is one of the many benefits of signing up for this service. You get a lot more than just the storage capacity with this, which means that the value is very fantastic and that you get a lot for that amount of money.

Gaining Access to OneDrive

OneDrive can be accessed by going to **onedrive.com**, where users can either log in with their current details or establish a new account by signing up for a free OneDrive account. Once you have signed in, you will be able to see all of the files that are accessible to you.

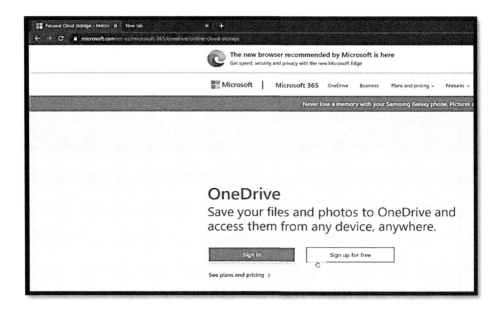

Much like other online Microsoft apps, you will have access to a menu on the left side of the screen. You can use this menu to explore the many options that are available to you.

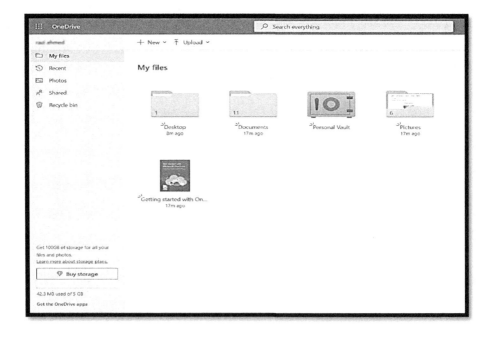

Additionally, in the top right corner of your OneDrive interface, you will see a selection of navigational choices that you can use. You might, for instance, display files by size, sort them by size, or rearrange them in a different order. You have the option to change the view that is being shown; for instance, you may choose the List view to see the date, the sharing status of the document, as well as the size of the file. You always have the option to go back to the Tiles view to obtain a preview of all of the documents that are currently accessible.

Getting familiar with the OneDrive Desktop User Interface

If you are using Windows or if you have already installed OneDrive, you should now see an icon that looks like a cloud in the bottom right-hand corner of your screen. This cloud symbol is the OneDrive icon.

You are provided with an update about the current status whenever you hover your mouse over the icon, and as a result, you can determine whether or not everything is presently up to date.

You can proceed and click on this button to learn more about the features that are available with OneDrive. To begin, one of the things that you will notice is up here at the top of this box that has shown, and that is that all of the information in your OneDrive account is updated. Let's say you just loaded a whole bunch of new pictures or documents onto your computer. It will show you the current status and it will tell you that it is currently updating.

You will see all of the files that have recently been synchronized on your computer just below that. When it comes to all of these files that have just been recently synced if you click on the ellipses over on the right-hand side, this reveals a few different actions that you can take on this file: you can open it to see what it is, you can share it with other people, you can view it online, and you can also look at the version history. We'll go through more of these options in a little while, but for now, our goal is to help you get used to the User experience of OneDrive Desktop and demonstrate how you can do a variety of operations on files that have just been synced to your account.

At the very bottom of the OneDrive app, there is a row of three buttons labeled "**Open**," "**See Online**," and "**Help and Settings**," each of which allows you to perform a different function. You can open the folder, view the content online, or access the Help and Settings menus. Now we're going to go through each one individually so you'll see precisely what it is that each one does.

To get things rolling, let's begin by selecting "**Open Folder**." This brings you to File Explorer, which displays all of the various directories and files that are currently stored on your computer. You will now see a folder for OneDrive in the top left corner of this screen. When you click on it, it will show you all of the different folders and files that you have stored in the cloud. When you put a folder or a file in the cloud, it backs it up, you can access it from anywhere, and you can also collaborate with other people on these files.

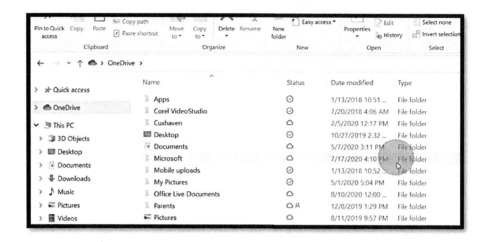

Let's take a moment and have a little conversation about what we can see from this view. You may first notice something a bit different from the standard view in File Explorer, and that is that you now have a column here that is named "**Status**. "

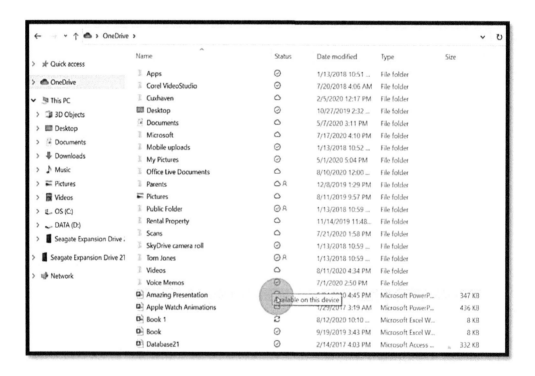

Let's take a quick tour of the meanings of these various symbols. If you ever find yourself curious about the significance of these icons or if you forget what they represent, all you have to do is hover over them, and you'll immediately be reminded of their significance. You can choose from a variety of icons here, such as the one that looks like a **green circle with a check mark** inside of it. That indicates that the file in question is not only stored on your PC but also in the cloud. The version of the file that is stored on your computer and the one that is stored in the cloud will always be the same if you use OneDrive since it will take care of keeping the files in sync for you.

If you look closely at some of your files, you may see an **icon** that looks like a **cloud**. This symbol represents a file that is now stored in the cloud; however, you do not have a local copy of the file on your computer. You may be questioning whether or not you can still open that file. If you have a file that is stored in the cloud but not on your computer, you can access it by clicking on the file, and it will immediately begin to download the file to your computer and then open it.

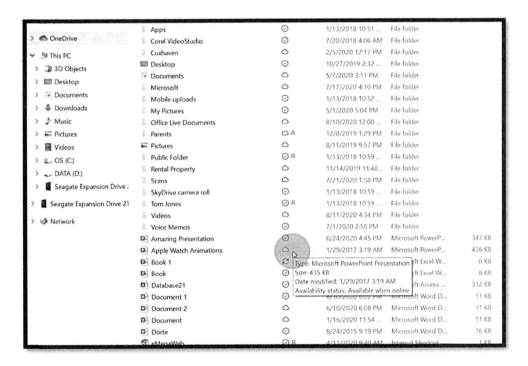

You also have a few other icons available here. Whenever you see a **person symbol**, it means that you are presently sharing this folder with other people; thus, it is a simple method to check if you have shared this with other people.

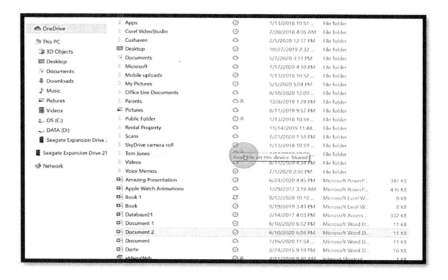

Additionally, if your file displays a **sync icon**, this indicates that OneDrive is in the process of synchronizing the file between your local computer and the cloud storage location.

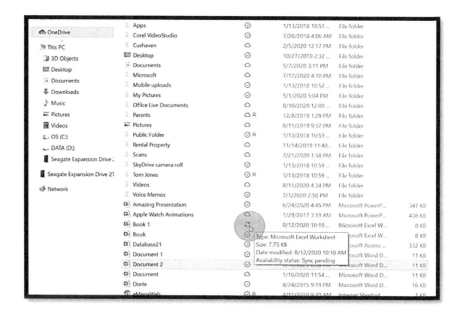

When you have a file or a folder on OneDrive, you have access to several different activities that you can do on that file. When you right-click on a file in this area, the context menu will appear. In Windows, you can generally do things like open the file, you can rename the file, and delete the file. However, since you are using OneDrive, you will also have access to five more activities in this menu. We are going to go over them, and in the end, you will have an idea of what you can do with them.

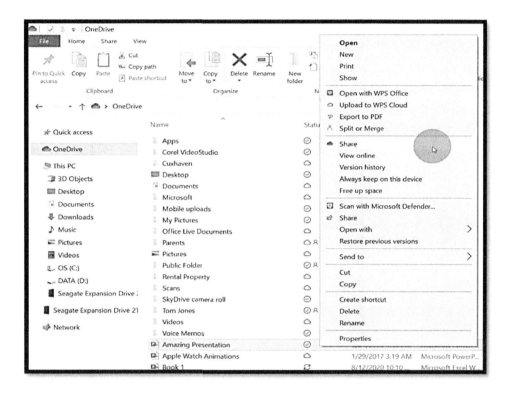

The first action is labeled "**Share**," and if you go ahead and click on this, the share window will be brought into view. You may recall that at the beginning of this chapter, we said that one of the advantages of utilizing OneDrive is that it makes it extremely simple to share and collaborate on files with other people. Now that you are here, one of the things you can do is send a link to someone else. If you click on this, you will be presented with some different control options. You have the option of allowing another person to edit the file alongside you, or you have the option of turning off editing, in which case they will still be able to view the file but they won't be able to make any changes to it.

If you have a paid subscription to Microsoft 365, you also get access to some additional options. For instance, if you only want someone to be able to edit it for the next couple of days, you can set an expiration date and then lock the file afterward. If you share something confidential, you can also set a password, and others will need to enter the password before they can open the file.

Back to the "**Share**" window, within this area, you can type in a name or an email address to share it with someone else, and then you can click on the "**Send**" button. As an alternative, you can also copy a link to this file, and then you can share it through some other method, such as WhatsApp or Facebook; therefore, you can share your document or your content through these means.

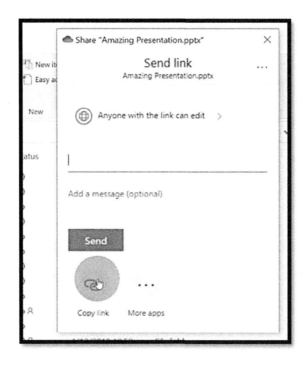

When you are back at the main screen, repeat the previous step of **right-clicking** on the file to bring up the **Context menu**. You also have the choice of **viewing the file online** if it is a Microsoft Word, Excel, or PowerPoint document. This is one of the other alternatives available to you. Should you choose to proceed and click on PowerPoint, the presentation will open in the online version of PowerPoint. PowerPoint on the web is completely free to use, and as a result, you can modify your files by logging in online and using PowerPoint.

You are going to right-click on the file once again after you have returned to the file explorer. You will have access to the **Version history** feature of OneDrive if you want to save your files there. If you go ahead and click on this, you get to see the history of that file. Now imagine that you are working with other people on a file, and someone makes some drastic edits that perhaps you don't agree with, and you want to go back to an earlier version of the file. You can very easily do that by clicking on the ellipses, and you can restore that version of the file. If you want to go back to an earlier version of the file, you can click on the ellipses again.

If you repeat the process of right-clicking on the file, the Context menu will pop up once again, and this time it will provide you with two more choices. The instruction "**Always keep on this device**" is one of them. You can go ahead and always keep a copy on your computer if you want the file to also be synced on your computer. For example, if you are going on a trip or you are going to be on a plane, where there will be no internet access, and you want the file to be synced on your computer, you can always keep a copy on your computer.

You also have the option of ensuring that the file remains in the cloud while not keeping a copy on your computer; in this instance, you will be able to free up some space on your device. This can be thought of as the reversal of the first option. You always have the option to "**Free up space**," so if you have a lot of movies that you've uploaded to OneDrive but don't want them to take up space on your hard drive, you can choose that option.

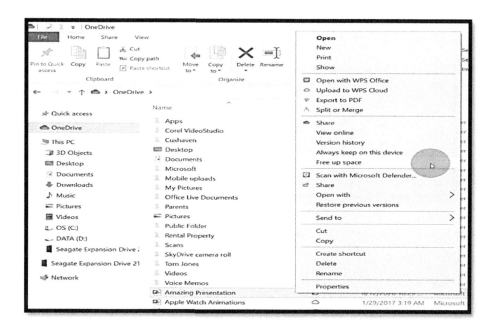

Using onedrive.com

You can also gain access to all of these files by opening your web browser, navigating to **onedrive.com**, logging in, or registering for an account there. Doing any of these things will provide you access to the aforementioned files.

After having a look at what the folder view is like, let's go back to the bottom right corner of the screen, and at this point, you are going to click on the OneDrive icon once again. Now that we've looked at what you can do inside the File Explorer or the "**Open folder**" view, let's see what you can do online by going ahead and clicking on "**View online**."

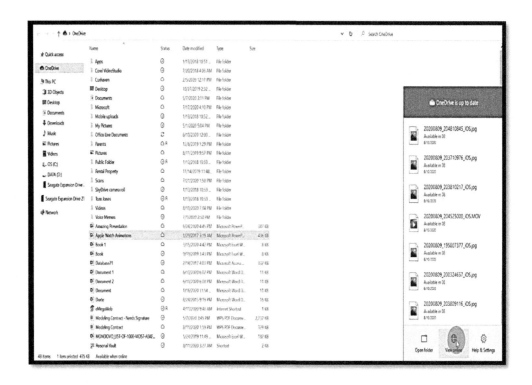

If you click on **"View online**," the OneDrive website will come up. On the OneDrive website, you will get a view that is similar to the one you had on your desktop, but it will also show you everything that is currently saved in the cloud. We are going to begin at the very top of the page and continue our way down to the bottom of the document. Microsoft has a highly powerful search engine that allows you to locate any files that you've uploaded to the cloud from this location. Therefore, when you enter in the name of a file, you will see that file appear in this section; this is an extremely efficient method for searching through all of the various files that you have saved on OneDrive.

By default, you will find yourself in the "**My files**" view, which is where we will remain until we discuss the contents of this particular view. You can generate new files within "**My files**." If you click on the "**New**" menu, you will be taken to a page where you can generate a new folder. In addition, you will have the ability to generate new versions of Word, Excel, PowerPoint, OneNote, Forms, and even plain text documents directly from this new menu. This is accomplished by utilizing the various Microsoft Office online applications.

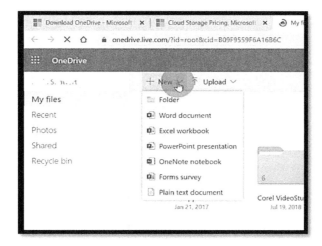

You have the option of not only generating a new file but also uploading data. If you have more files or folders that you want to place on OneDrive but you do not intend to simply sync them on your computer, you can come straight to OneDrive and then upload them here. As an example, let's imagine that you have other files or folders that you want to put on OneDrive. If you upload a file to OneDrive from this location, and you switch to the File Explorer view, you'll see that the file you uploaded has also been uploaded to File Explorer.

The good news is that any changes you make to files stored in the OneDrive folder on your personal computer, as well as any changes you make to files stored in the OneDrive folder on the web, will result in those changes being made on both locations, giving you access to your files from anywhere.

Let's have a look at some of the options available under the "**My files**" area of the application. Over on the right-hand side of the screen, you'll find some additional sorting options. These are very similar to the ones found in File Explorer, where you can arrange items according to their names, the dates on which they were most recently modified, the sizes of those modifications, and a variety of other criteria.

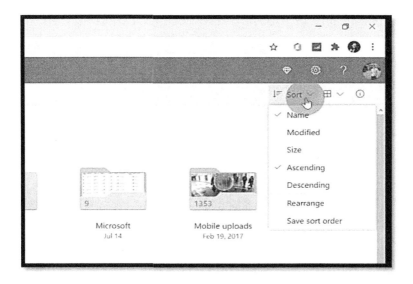

In addition to categorizing, you also have the option of visualizing the files in a variety of various ways. So, let's suppose you want to see a compact list, but if you think you may be more comfortable with the tiles view, you can change the view to reflect what you think will be most helpful to you.

Additionally, in the top right-hand corner of the screen, there is a circle with the letter I inside of it. If you click on it, an activity view will appear, which will show you all of the actions that have taken place inside your OneDrive as well as on the different files.

You have all of these different controls for visualizing and checking your activity, and below that, you see all of your folders exactly as they appeared within File Explorer; however, now you can access all of them on the web, and just like on your desktop, you can also take actions on these files.

When you right-click on a file, a Context menu will appear. This menu, similar to File Explorer on the desktop, will allow you to do a variety of operations on the selected file. For example, you can open the file, can share it with other people (if you click on share, this will bring up a sharing dialogue that is comparable to what you had on the desktop), and you also have access to the version history of the file; therefore, very similar actions to those that you can perform directly within Windows can also be performed directly from the web.

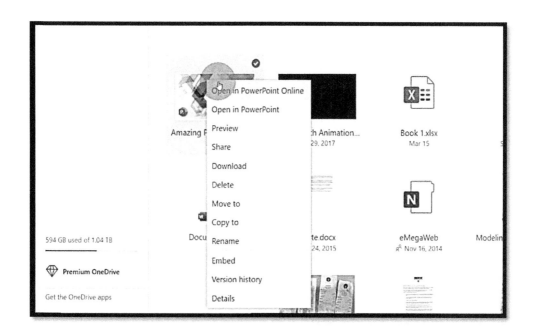

Now, there is one more object that appears here, and it seems fascinating. It's called the **Personal Vault**, and it looks like a large safe or a vault.

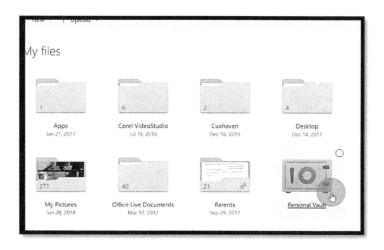

Within OneDrive is a specialized folder that you can use to store files, and the purpose of this folder is to store items for which you want to ensure that their safety is maintained to the highest possible degree. You have the option of enabling two-factor authentication, which means that in addition to logging in to OneDrive to access it, you will typically also be required to either get a code sent to your email or type in a code that appears on your phone and then enter that code to gain access to the Personal Vault. You can enable two-factor authentication by going to the Personal Vault settings and selecting the Authentication tab. If, for example, you have a picture of your driver's license or even your social security card, rather than simply storing it in one of the standard folders that come with OneDrive, you should store it in the Personal Vault because it is a more secure location for storing materials of this nature. It is an additional layer of security designed to keep things extremely secure.

After having a look at the Files view, let's go over to the left-hand side and see what other options you have available to you. There is also a view called **"Recent,"** which displays all of the most recent documents you worked on. This provides you with an overview of what you have been working on most recently and assists you in returning to what is most important to you.

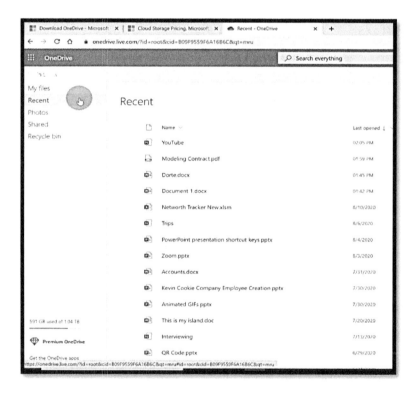

Below that, you also have a **"Photos"** view, and if you click on that, within photos, you see a bunch of photos appearing. You can also click into Albums, and you can see photos arranged by place. Then, once again, just like within the other view, you have different filtering options that you can pull up here, and you can also pull up activity that's recently happened within your photos view.

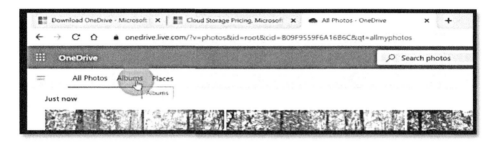

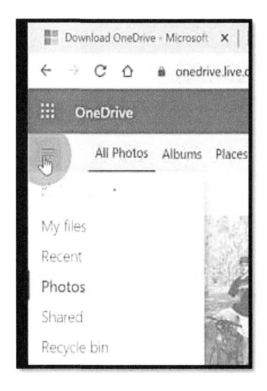

If you go back to the left-hand side of the page and click on the hamburger menu, you will see the collection of files that you have **shared** with other users over time.

Last but not least, if you go to the **"Recycle Bin"** and click on it, you will be able to see any items that you have previously removed but now want to restore. You should be aware that they will remain in the Recycle Bin for a certain length of time before they are removed permanently; nonetheless, this provides you with the option to recover files if you deleted them inadvertently.

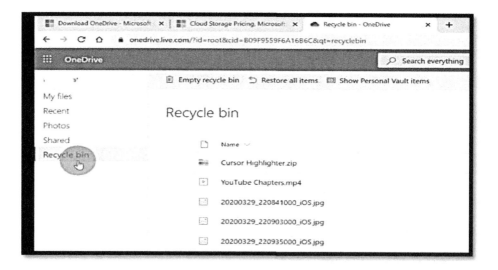

Now that we have examined the web interface, let's go back to the OneDrive icon that is located down here in the bottom right-hand corner. You are going to click on this once more, and the last one that you want to click on is the one that is titled **"Help & Settings."** This opens up a menu that contains various options, and you are going to click on the one that says **"Settings."**

There are a few things to keep you interested while you're exploring the "**Settings**" menu. You can get started by clicking on the **Settings** tab that is located at the very top of the screen. Once you are there, one of the options that you will see is that you can choose to have OneDrive automatically start when you start Windows. If you choose to have this option enabled, then any new files that you create will be automatically synced with the cloud. Down below, there's another option that says "**Save space and download files as you use them**." This means that if you create a file, rather than keeping it on your computer and taking up space, you can instead make it be only on OneDrive. When you interact with that file, it will download a copy, but once you're finished with it, it will make sure the file is stored in the cloud. You will be able to free up some space on your computer as a result of this, and you will also have the peace of mind of knowing that Microsoft is backing it up and will have it ready for you whenever you may want it in the future.

Next, you will want to click on the **"Account"** tab that is located at the very top of the window. Here, one of the things you will notice is that you will have the ability to choose the folders that Microsoft OneDrive will sync.

To do this, simply click on the **"Choose folders"** option, and then you will have the opportunity to define which folders will be synced.

Next, there is another option that is labeled **"Backup,"** and if you click on it, you will be brought to a screen where you can specify the essential folder that will be backed up by OneDrive. If you have stuff saved to your desktop, the Documents folder on your computer, or the Pictures folder on your computer, clicking the **"Manage backup"** button will cause all of those locations to be synchronized with your OneDrive folder.

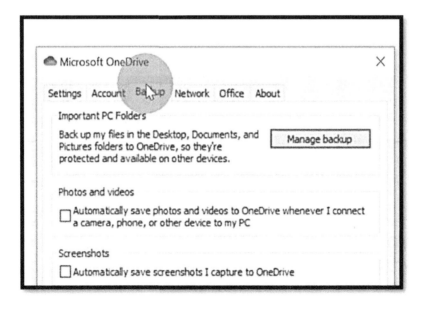

You also have the option of configuring OneDrive in such a way that any new photos or videos that you add to your computer will immediately be uploaded to OneDrive. This can be done manually or automatically, depending on your preference.

Features of OneDrive you would benefit from

What are some of the most interesting and useful aspects of OneDrive that you can make use of?

The ability to **create and modify documents** in Microsoft Office for free is by far the most significant benefit here. To begin editing Microsoft Office documents stored in OneDrive, you do not need any extra licenses of any kind.

Accessing files on mobile devices is another significant one. You are not limited to accessing files on your desktop computer, Mac, or Windows operating system; rather, you can also download applications on your iPhone or Android device and view your files from there.

You also receive **free storage** of up to 5 GB, which, when you put it in perspective like that, is a significant amount of space. You can save a large number of Word documents and pictures in that free area, making it possible for you to immediately begin utilizing it without incurring any more expenses.

Since you can make edits to documents created in Microsoft Office, you are also able to **share and collaborate** on Microsoft Office files with other people. You can create a document on OneDrive, share the link with the other individuals working on the project with you, and then work on the project collectively. This works particularly well if you are working on a project with a group of people.

Let's take a look at how you can collaborate on the same document in OneDrive while also sharing files with other people. To do this, open a new document in Word by selecting the **"New"** button.

Now that you have a new file and have decided on a topic for your project, all that is left to do is give this document a name. After that, you can go to the following step, which is to click the **"Share"** button and then email this document to another person. You will get a notification that your email was successfully delivered, at which point both of you will be able to collaborate on the same document.

When you and another person are collaborating on a document stored in OneDrive, you will be able to see the changes made by the other person in real-time. To illustrate this point, let us suppose that you have already composed the first paragraph of your document, but that in addition to you, someone else will be making revisions to it. Therefore, you will be able to view the adjustments that they've made, as well as the individuals who made the changes.

Because the adjustments are almost immediate, you won't even require complex technology to collaborate effectively with this method. For instance, you and your coworker may carry on a conversation over the phone while simultaneously making changes to the document, and you will both be able to see those changes in real-time.

Exploring on your own

To gain mastery of all you have learned in this chapter, it's time to explore on your own by carrying out the following activities:

- Install and sign up for a free or premium plan OneDrive account on your computer
- Download and install OneDrive on your Mobile device and ensure you are signed in
- Start creating and uploading files using any of the means and confirm that your account is synchronized across all your devices
- Practice sharing a file with a friend or colleague and work together with that person to see how the collaboration system works

CHAPTER 2

WORKING WITH ONEDRIVE ONLINE

OneDrive is already integrated with some of Microsoft's productivity and communication tools, such as Skype and Outlook, so if you currently use them, you can immediately start using OneDrive. The sign-in process for Microsoft Suite is identical to that of Google Suite; users just need one account for all of Microsoft's products. There is no need for concern if you have never used Microsoft products and so do not have an account with them. In this chapter, we are going to cover how you can work with OneDrive Online. We will start with how you can sign up for an account, then understand the Interface, and end with how you can automatically sync your OneDrive files.

Signing up to OneDrive

You can get started with OneDrive by going to the website's official URL, which is **microsoft.com/OneDrive**, and registering using your email address. You can use any email service you like, including Gmail, Outlook, or Yahoo! Just make sure that the email address you provide is still active since you will be required to validate your new Microsoft account via the use of a link that will be sent to the email address you use.

Create a password for yourself, and make it a priority to keep it as safe as you possibly can. Once your account has been validated, you will be able to continue using OneDrive itself.

You should be aware of this fact if you use a personal computer operating under the Windows 10 operating system: the OneDrive desktop application will already be pre-installed on your computer. You can access the OneDrive icon by navigating to the bottom right of the taskbar and clicking on the arrow that appears there. Simply follow the steps outlined in the previous paragraph once you have clicked on it if you do not already have an account.

If you have a Mac, you also have the option to download the desktop program and utilize it instead, if you find that to be a more convenient option.

Let's get started with OneDrive straight away, shall we, now that you've successfully finished the signup process?

Signing into your account

Simply entering onedrive.live.com into your browser's address bar will take you to the sign-up page for the OneDrive service, where you can log into your account. You can now go ahead and sign in using the free account that you created, and when you go to the next page, all you have to do is enter your password and click the 'Sign in' button. After that, it will lead you to OneDrive. The cloud is going to be used as the location for storing all of the information that you provide.

The Online Interface

The user interface of OneDrive Online is quite straightforward and uncomplicated. The use of blue and white in the design makes it simple and easy for the eyes. We're going to take things nice and slow so that you can become acquainted with OneDrive, but you're welcome to experiment with it and find out where its functional capabilities end. You can see how OneDrive combines the rest of the Microsoft Suite by clicking on the symbol that looks like a square with dots inside of it, which is located in the upper left corner of the app.

If you are already subscribed to the subscription version of Microsoft 365, you can easily work on your documents, sheets, and presentations across the many platforms that are included in the Suite. You can also share, modify, and give access as you see fit. It is a pretty handy setup. In the menu, you will discover connections to OneNote, Excel, and PowerPoint, as well as Teams, To-Do, and Outlook, among other applications.

You can access your files by selecting the **"My Files"** tab located on the same dashboard. When you first log in to your OneDrive, you will be brought to this screen automatically. You will be able to locate the files that you have uploaded to the cloud for storage purposes here.

You should be aware that OneDrive provides free storage with a total capacity of 5 GB if you have recently registered a Microsoft account. If you have not upgraded to any of the premium or business plans, then you will remain on the free plan automatically for as long as you have not upgraded. You'll be able to verify this information by looking in the far-left corner of the blue dashboard.

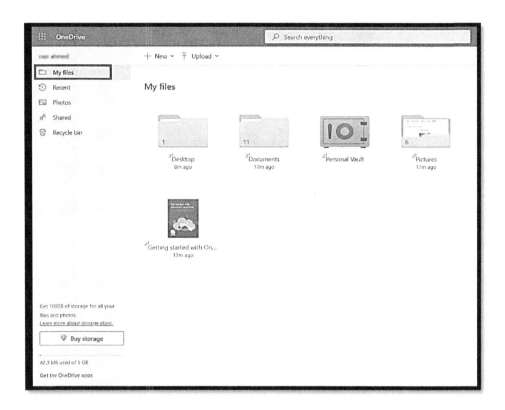

There, if you click the link that says **"Buy Storage**," it will lead you to a website where you can choose one of several different premia plans that OneDrive offers.

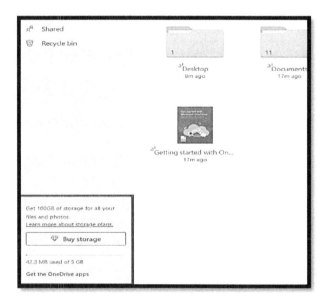

You are now subscribed to the free plan, which gives you a total of only 5 GB of storage space. If you want more, you'll have to sign up for a plan that's geared for businesses or individuals, depending on what you need. Be sure to thoroughly examine each of the plans by clicking on the "**Go Premium**" link, and choose the one that is the best fit for your requirements. There are at least eight distinct plans that can be selected, so you must investigate the characteristics of each option before settling on the one that is most suitable for you. You are only allowed to upload a maximum of three files to the Personal Vault if you are using a free subscription.

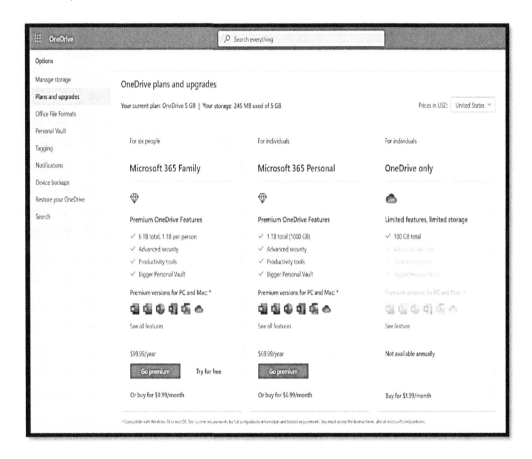

You can check exactly how much of the free 5 GB of space is still available to you to use by clicking on the little symbol that can be seen just under the link that says "**Go Premium**."

You will see two buttons labeled **"New"** and **"Upload"** in the upper left-hand corner of the page that is titled **"My Files."**

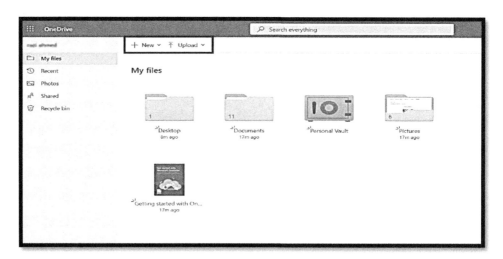

Using the **"New"** button, you can create new folders inside the Suite, in addition to generating documents of any sort. If you are using a browser, selecting the link to create a new document will cause a new tab to be created in the browser. Bear in mind that whatever you do on the new page synchronizes immediately with OneDrive, and if you go back to "**My Files**," you'll be able to access everything there.

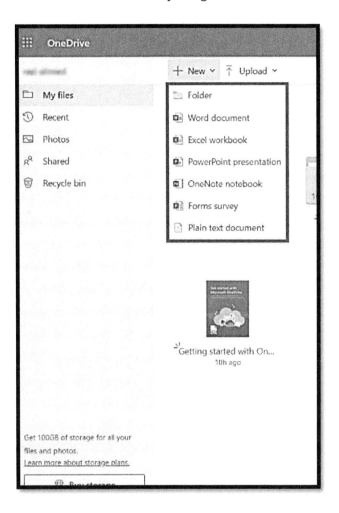

Within "**My Files**," there is a unique section known as the "**Personal Vault**." It is a password-protected portion of your OneDrive cloud storage that offers you the highest level of protection for storing even the most sensitive information, including media files. There is a two-step verification process, and the account will get locked after a maximum of 20 minutes of inactivity on the user's part. Additionally, you get access to it from any device on which you log in to OneDrive, including your mobile phone.

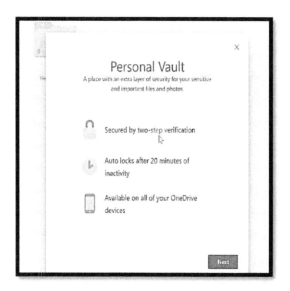

After you have clicked on it, you will be required to provide a secondary email address or a phone number so that a unique verification code can be delivered to either one of those places. Once this code has been entered and the user has returned to the first screen, the vault will be accessible. You may get an error notice claiming that the verification attempt failed; however, if you refresh the page, everything will return to its usual state. You should be aware that the Vault cannot store all documents.

Now that we've circled back around to the main dashboard, the "**Recent**" link is the one that comes next. You'll be able to locate and make changes to all of the files you've recently accessed and updated in this section.

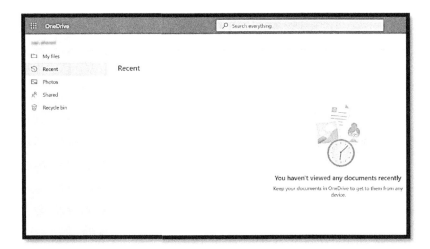

The "**Photos**" link is the next thing to be shown on the main dashboard. This folder, which is located on your cloud storage, stores all of the images that you have uploaded to it. Because the cloud storage has its built-in picture viewer, you can access your images and open them immediately from the cloud. The pictures are arranged in groups according to the album, the tags, and the places.

Following that is the "**Shared**" area, in which you will be able to examine the content that you have either shared with other users or to which you have authorized access to a third party.

The fourth area is referred to as the "**Recycle Bin**," and its role is well-known to everyone familiar with even the most fundamental aspects of how a computer, including mobile devices, operates.

You can also upload locally stored files to your OneDrive account. The uploading process is rather simple. You just need to go to the file or media that you want to upload on your device, click the **"Upload"** button, and then choose it from the menu that appears when you do so. Simply clicking on it will upload your work to the cloud, where it will be secured from loss.

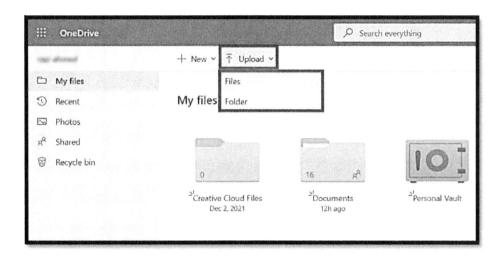

There are **four icons** located in the upper right corner of the main screen.

The first is a link to subscribe to the **premium** service.

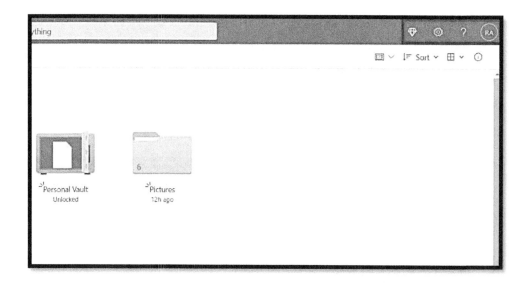

The second icon is for the **settings**, and here is where you can make changes to the language that you speak as well as access other features like device backups and notifications.

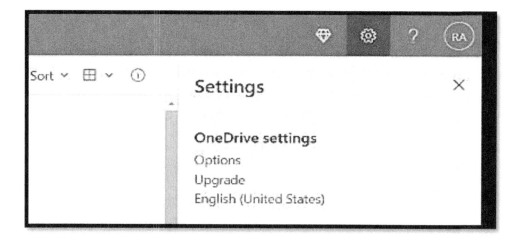

The third icon is labeled with the word "**Help**." Because it is in the form of a question mark, it is impossible to overlook. There is a section devoted to frequently asked questions that includes a list of concerns, such as what it means when your account is locked and how to solve sync issues with OneDrive. You can also contact support and report a complaint using the same window.

You can access your Microsoft OneDrive profile by selecting the fourth symbol here. From this section, you can also sign out of your OneDrive account.

You'll note that to open a file, you need to double-click. If you click once on a file, specifically the small circle in the top right corner of each file icon, a list of options will appear at the top of the page. These options include **Open**, **Share**, **Download**, **Delete**, **Move To**, **Copy**, **Rename**, **Embed**, and **Version History**. You can also view the version history of a file.

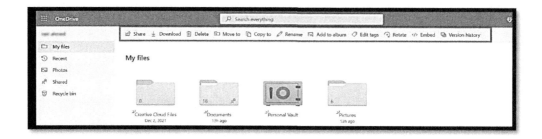

Any one of these settings can be set to make a file readable or executable, and any one of these choices can be applied to any one of these files. You can also designate numerous files and documents to be run in whichever manner you see fit by making use of the little white circle.

Automatic Syncing

You should also be familiar with the process of setting up a location on your computer that is capable of automatically syncing the files with your OneDrive outline. This will cause it to take all of the files from a particular location on your file and upload them to OneDrive in the manner previously described.

You can do this by clicking the link that says **"Get the OneDrive applications"** that is located in the bottom left corner of the screen.

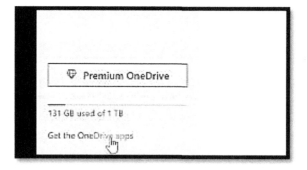

You are going to just click on it, and if you are using Windows 10, you should already have it installed on your computer. However, if you do not already have it installed on your computer, you can go through the download process and install it on your computer. This will also function well on your Mac.

Right at this moment, you are going to click the **"Start OneDrive"** button, and then you are going to hit the **"Open"** button.

At this point, all you need to do is enter your address and sign in for it to go through and connect.

Your folders in OneDrive will become accessible after you do this. If you click on your OneDrive and simultaneously open up this folder, you will see that the contents stored here are the same ones that are on your OneDrive, and you will also notice that everything is beginning to sync. Additionally, if you see the green check mark right here, it indicates that it has already been synchronized, which means that it is present in both locations, namely on your local computer as well as in the cloud. If it just shows the Cloud, this indicates that it is only stored in the Cloud and that it has not yet synchronized, however, if it shows a double arrow, it indicates that it is now in the process of syncing.

You will notice that you have these Clouds if you go down when you're in Windows and look at this section. They may be hiding in your Hidden Icons folder. If you want to view them a little bit faster, you can drag them onto your taskbar. If it is synchronizing, you will notice that it is not blue yet; clicking on it will show you what is occurring. If you choose **"View online,"** you will just be sent back to the online version of OneDrive.

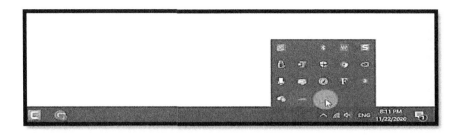

If you choose to open the folder, anything you save inside of it will automatically be uploaded to your OneDrive account. For instance, if you copy a file from your computer and drop it into your OneDrive Personal, the file will be copied into that location, and at that moment, it will say that it is syncing because it is going through, and when that becomes a green check mark, that will show up over your OneDrive Online; therefore, if you refresh it, you will be able to determine whether or not it has synced yet.

Keep in mind that whatever you save in the personal folder of your OneDrive will automatically be uploaded to the Online version of your OneDrive, where it will be accessible to you.

You can now see that you have several different options available to you if you right-click on any of the files that are located in the personal folder of your OneDrive.

This is the location where you can work from the online environment as well as on your personal computer. When you install this on a computer, it will bring all of your information from your OneDrive. If you install this on three or four different computers, it will sync all of these different ones up, which means that you will have your information living in different places. If this is what you want, then it is fine to do so as long as you have enough space for it.

Exploring on your own

To gain mastery of all you have learned in this chapter, it's time to explore on your own by carrying out the following activities:

- Sign in to OneDrive Online and master the interface.
- Set up OneDrive App on your computer as you've learned in this chapter.

CHAPTER 3

WORKING WITH FILES AND FOLDERS

In this chapter, we are going to walk you through the process of creating some folders and files, and then you will know how to upload some folders and files from your personal computer into your OneDrive account.

Creating a new Folder

There are a few distinct approaches one can take to create a new folder on their computer.

When you right-click anywhere in **"My files,"** the **"New"** option will become available to you. You can upload files and folders at this location.

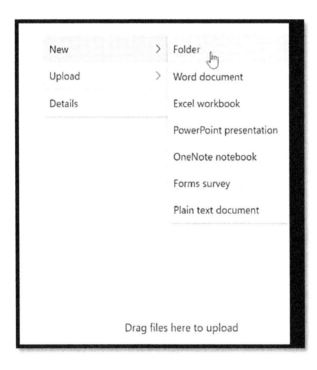

Within **"My files,"** you will also see the **"New"** option right at the top. Therefore, any approach is acceptable.

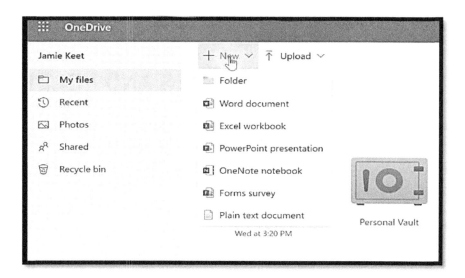

Now that you are ready, you can **create a folder** by selecting one of the available methods, navigating to the **"Folder"** menu option, naming the folder, and selecting the **"Create"** button.

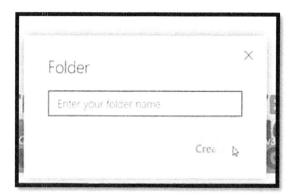

Moving Folders

You can arrange your files in any way that you see fit, which includes creating more folders and subfolders as well as moving existing ones around. You are not limited in the number of folders or subfolders that you can create. To do this, just **click** the folder you wish to move, then hold down the mouse button and **drag** it to the location you choose. This will move the folder to the new location.

If you transfer that folder into another folder, then when you open the new folder, you will be able to view the subfolder that you just moved within the original folder. You can also see how these files are grouped by looking in the upper left corner of the screen. Once you do so, you can click on various portions to go back through the levels. One option to move your folders is to use this method.

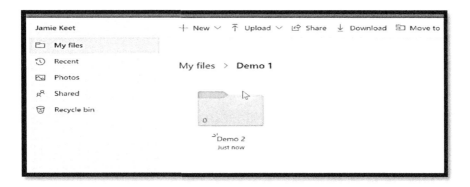

You can also move straight from here if you right-click on a folder. This is another option. If you **right-click** and choose **"Move to,"** then it will ask you where you want to move it to, and then it will move it there.

If you want to move it inside of **"Documents,"** for example, you can click and it will move it there.

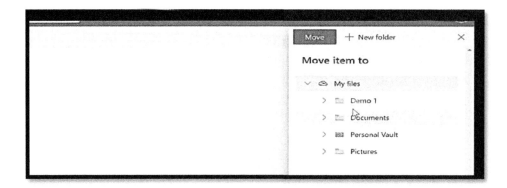

Once you have chosen the new place, go to the top of the page and click the "**Move**" button. This will move it to the new position. In summary, to move your folders, you can either **drag** them or use the **right-click** menu on your mouse.

Creating a file

The second thing we are discussing is how to create a file from inside a folder that you already have. If you like using Microsoft products, you will be pleased to learn that you have access to online versions of Microsoft Word, Microsoft Powerpoint, and Microsoft Excel.

You can see that you have documents in Word, Excel, Powerpoint, Onenote, Forms, and Plain text if you go ahead and right-click and then choose "**New**" from the menu that appears.

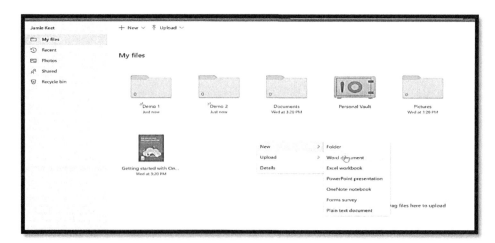

You are going to go ahead and click on "**Word document**" here, and when you do so, what will pop up is the online version of Microsoft Word. If you're familiar with Google, this would be the same as a Google Doc, and you could even find it to be more substantial than Google documents.

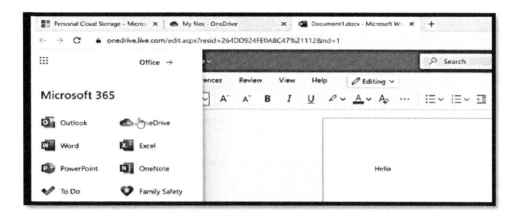

On the other hand, you can do more things with it since it's closer to what the app is. You are free to begin typing in this area, and if you ever need to return to OneDrive, just click the app launcher, then choose OneDrive from the menu that appears. You have the option of going back to OneDrive using this method, or you can simply switch the tab over, in which case you will see that the Word document has been loaded here. If you haven't given it a name yet but would want to, you can give it one by right-clicking on it, selecting "**Rename**," and then selecting "**Save**."

Moving Files

You can move this, just as you did with the folders. It's all up to you. If you want to move a file, all you have to do is **click** and **drag** it to a different folder. Once you do so, you'll see that it has migrated from its previous place to the new folder, and it is now in the location you specified.

Another thing to mention is that when you choose a file, you will see a row of options at the top of the window. These options will allow you to delete, move, copy, rename, and download the file, among other things.

The same thing occurs when you right-click on that file; you get all of the various choices that you can do, and we'll speak about a couple more of them as we go along with you here to ensure that you are familiar with how to interact with all of these different file kinds.

You have the option of creating more documents, and this time it could be a presentation using Powerpoint. You then navigate to your Powerpoint presentation, enter the details of your file, and at the very top, you have the option to change the name from Presentation to any name you want.

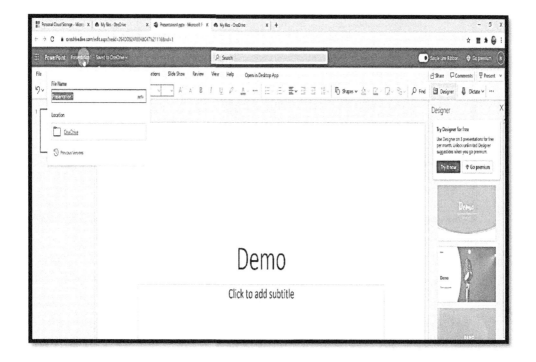

When you are finished, you simply navigate back to your OneDrive files, where the file will be visible, and you can then move it to the location of your choice to keep things organized.

Uploading Files and Folders

The next step is when you have certain files on your computer such as PDFs, PowerPoint presentations, or Word documents, and you wish to upload them to OneDrive. You can right-click anywhere and then go to the **"Upload files or folders"** option to upload files or folders. You can upload it by going into your folders and doing so, but keep in mind that you can also change the directories around.

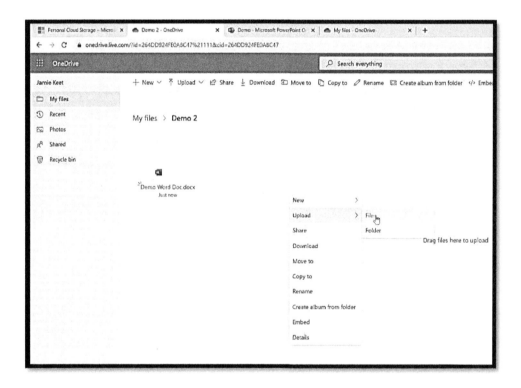

You will right-click inside of a folder, go to the **"Upload"** menu option, and then choose a file to upload this time. This will open your File Explorer so that you can choose the document that you wish to upload. Even if you created the document with your Microsoft application, you can still access it and it will open online. Later on, you will learn how you can link your app; if you are using Microsoft or PowerPoint, you can connect it to

OneDrive so that it automatically saves your work there, and you can also continue to work on your applications during this time.

Photos

Simply uploading your images to OneDrive in the same way that you upload all of your other folders and files is all that is required for them to appear in the Photos tab of your OneDrive account. You can upload items by simply clicking the **"Upload"** link or right-clicking, exactly as you saw before. However, you can also drag things directly over from your computer, and as you'll see, the picture will now be shown here. It is important to remember that you can do this with any of the other files as well.

You may repeat this process as many times as you want by grabbing another one, dragging it across, and then dropping it into your OneDrive folder. You didn't put them directly in Photos, but after refreshing, you can see that they are now there. OneDrive is aware that these are photographs, so what will happen if you go to the **"Photos"** section now is that you will notice that they are loading up in this section.

You should also take note that in the upper right corner of this window, you have the option to **"Show photos"** either from All files or from Pictures folders.

You can move them as well if you go back to your files; you can right-click on any of the photos, and if you want to move many pictures at once, you can pick as many pictures as you want, and when you're done, you go to the menu and choose **"Move**." After that, you would go to the "**Pictures**" tab and choose "**Move**".

Now, what you'll see is that they are not appearing in your OneDrive; rather, they have been transferred to the Pictures folder that can be found in this location. If you go back over to the Photos tab, what you will see displayed at first is your images from the "**All**" folders; alternatively, you can only go to your "**Pictures**" folder, but the contents will be the same since you transferred those pictures over. When you do many of these simultaneously, it could help you save time by avoiding the need to do each task individually.

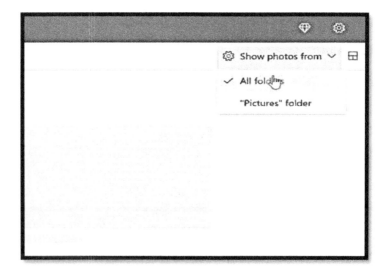

It is important to keep in mind that, just as you can drag your files over to OneDrive, and they will upload, you can also do the same thing with an entire folder by simply dragging it over, and it will be there as well, now uploaded along with all of the content that was previously contained within that folder. Everything is safe in OneDrive, and you have a copy of it stored elsewhere, so the process of transferring files is as simple as dragging and dropping them. You can accomplish this with both your photos and your documents.

You can also work with things online just as you do in the app if you're using Microsoft Word, Excel, and PowerPoint just like you did previously. You only need to double-click on the file, and it will automatically start opening in an internet browser for you.

Downloading a file from OneDrive

Additionally, you can download any of your files. You are already familiar with uploading and creating, but if you right-click on any of these, you will see that there is an option to download. If you right-click on any of them, you will see that there is an option to download; therefore, if you want to download to your computer, you can click on that file and then click **"Download."** You are already familiar with uploading and creating, but if you right-click on any of these, you will see that there is an option to download.

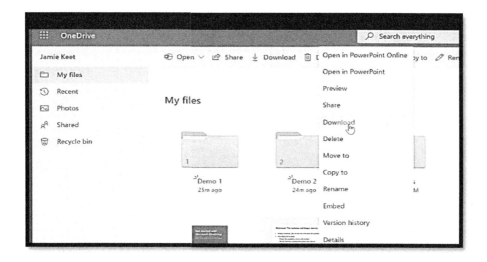

Once again, you can pick numerous items for download. You will notice that if you choose a few different ones (such as distinct files and folders), you can do different things to it. For example, you can delete them, move them, and share them with other people. However, if you go into a folder and choose many files here, you will have the option to download them. When you click **"Download**," they will zip the files up for you automatically. Keep in mind that when you have multiple ones that you've selected together to download, they will compress it and have it displayed as a OneDrive zip. However, you can go ahead and click on it and it will open up where you can extract it from here and then open those files here. This is something that you should keep in mind.

Organizing data on your drive

How would you recommend organizing all of the data that is stored on your drive? Whether you're a student or an employee, organizing the data on your drive in a hierarchical structure could be one of the most effective strategies to get everything in order. Using the image that can be seen below as an example, what you see here is forty years' worth of the hierarchical structure of the college, semesters, courses, and lectures. In the given scenario, the student at the technical college who is currently enrolled in studies has two semesters (Fall of 2020 and then spring of 2021). In the fall of 2020, the student will be taking two classes: Introduction to Computing and Windows 10. For the first class, Introduction to Computing, he will have two lectures (one on September 2nd and another lecture on September 9th). In the spring of 2021, he is only been required to take one subject (Soft Skills), but the lectures for this class had not been recorded yet.

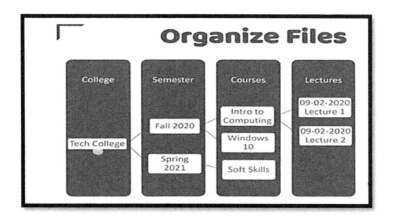

Now, how would you recommend organizing all of this information inside OneDrive? Because the names of the lectures are very similar, you can simply copy the name of the lecture, and when you create a new folder, you can just paste it and change only the lecture ID. The first step is to create a top folder that we will refer to as Technical College. We will then build the rest of the hierarchy by creating subfolders inside the original folders that we have created.

As you can see, the process of constructing this structure is shown here as a hierarchy. It begins with "My files," then moves on to "Technical college," then to "Fall 2020," and last to "Introduction to computers section." Within this folder, you will find the two lectures.

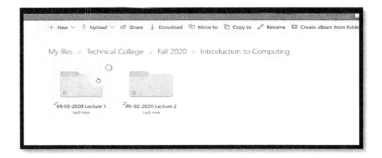

To move about inside this structure, you only need to click on the specific folder, and you will be brought back to the previous level. Simply clicking on the actual folder will take you within the hierarchy; this can be done by selecting the folder in question first.

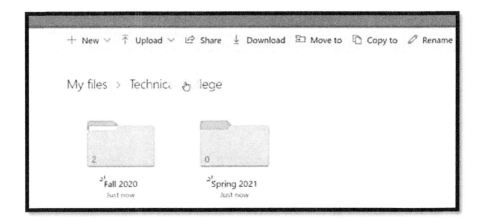

Now that you know how to construct the structure, let's look at how you can utilize it to make the most of all the advantages that OneDrive has to offer by referring to the earlier example. As soon as you have the framework in place, you can go to the lecture that will take place on September 2nd, create a new word document at this location, and then take notes throughout the presentation. To do this, just choose **"Word document"** from the drop-down menu that appears after clicking the **"New"** button.

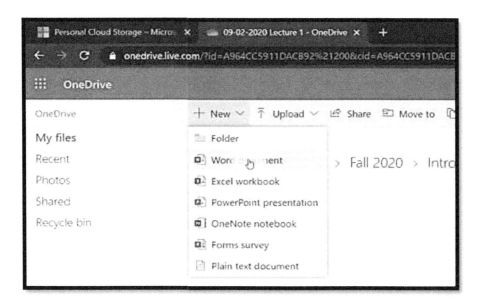

When you do that, it will take you to the online version of Word and start the creation of a completely new document in Word. As you can see, you also have the option of creating an Excel spreadsheet, a PowerPoint presentation, a notebook in OneNote, a survey form, or even just a plain text document. The most exciting aspect of this is that everything you create will be stored in the cloud, which means that you will be able to access it from any of your devices. Let's imagine that the classroom you were in did not have an internet connection; hence, you needed to take notes throughout the lesson using the offline mode, and you saved the file directly on your desktop. You can still upload the file that you made into OneDrive by following these steps: select the **"Upload"** button, go to the file that you created, and click.

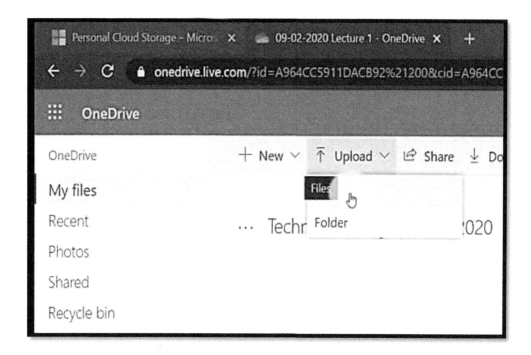

You can upload not just individual files but also the complete folder, which means that you will be able to bring in and recreate the structure directly from your desktop. This is another wonderful function that this platform offers.

Collaborating with others

The simplicity with which one can collaborate with other users is a key component of the Cloud's impressive capability. For example, if you have a PowerPoint presentation that you've uploaded and you want other people to work on it as well, you can share it with them and give them the appropriate permission to work on it

Sharing Files

You can share a file by selecting it, then clicking **"Share"** at the top of the screen, or you can just right-click on the file in question and pick **"Share"** from the context menu.

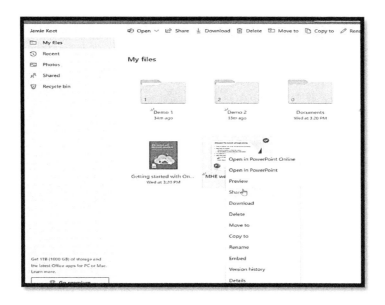

You should now be able to see the message "**Anyone with the link can edit**." You can type in the person's email address right here, as well as a message, and then click the "**Send**" button.

However, if they want to edit it, they will need at least an online PowerPoint account as well. In addition, they will need a OneDrive account to be able to edit anything associated with that.

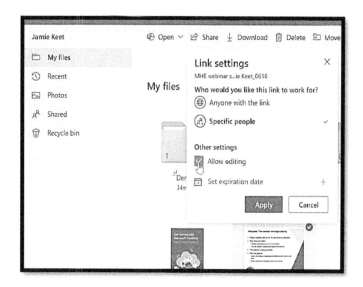

Changing Permissions

You can also adjust the permissions, so if you only want certain individuals to be able to edit that document, you can choose the corresponding option and then click the **"Apply"** button. After that, you go back to the section of the page where you can add individuals and enter their email addresses.

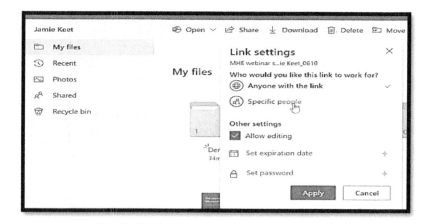

Additionally, if you do not want to permit editing, you can simply check this off, and then they will not be able to edit the document. If you see any of these options, such as **"Set expiry date"** or a password that has a small star symbol next to it, that means the account in question is a premium account. If you have a free account, you won't be able to do that; however, you can still do some sharing.

Sharing files via link

After applying the changes that you made, you also have the option to **copy the link** here and send it to an email. Alternatively, you can just type in the email addresses of the individuals that you want to notify, then click **"Send,"** and you will be informed from that account. That is all there is to sharing, and keep in mind that you can do that with everything; you can do that at the file level, you can right-click on a folder and share an entire folder out with people too, but the thing to keep in mind is that if you share the folder, anything you put in that folder gets shared out too, so make sure you know exactly what you're sharing and whether or not you want people to be able to edit the documents that you share with them.

Exploring on your own

To gain mastery of all you have learned in this chapter, it's time to explore on your own by carrying out the following activities:

- Create a new folder
- Create or upload a file such as Word, PowerPoint, Excel, or just a plain document.
- Move files and folders within your space using the methods you've learned in this chapter
- Create or upload a new folder and organize that folder as you saw in this chapter
- Share files and folders using the methods shown, and manage permissions of these files to see how it works.

CHAPTER 4

USING ONEDRIVE MOBILE ON YOUR PHONE

Now that we are in File Explorer and you can see all of your files, you may be asking what you should do if you want to view these files when you are away from your computer in another location. Earlier, we said that it is possible to acquire OneDrive on your mobile phone, and in just a minute, you will see how you can utilize OneDrive on your phone.

Getting Started

After discussing how you can use OneDrive on your personal computer as well as over the web, let's move on to discussing how you can use OneDrive after you've installed it on your mobile device. Let's get right into it if you have OneDrive already opened on your phone; that way, you can see some of the options that are available here. When you initially launch the app, you will be taken to the main OneDrive view (as seen in the following image), and here, too, you will see your file's view alongside all of the other files that you see on your computer's desktop as well as any files that you viewed on the internet.

On the desktop, as well as on the web, you can see all of your most recently saved files. To clarify, selecting **"Recent"** will bring up the list of recently accessed items.

You can access all of the files that you have **shared** with other people by clicking on the button that is located over on the right side of the screen, and once again, this view is quite similar to the one that you saw on the website.

After that, if you go to the tab labeled Photos, you will see all of the most recent pictures that you have taken with your mobile device.

You can record information with the OneDrive app on your phone, which is one of the many advantages of using this app. To do this, locate the picture symbol in the bottom-middle of the screen; tapping on it will bring up the camera application.

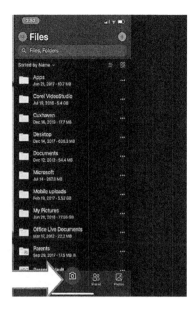

Now, what you can do is take images of documents, and you can also take pictures of whiteboards; it does an excellent job of capturing content.

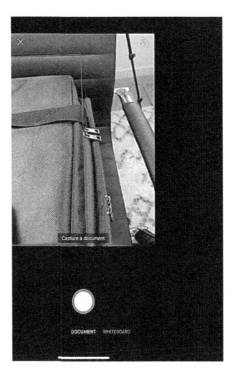

You also have the option of clicking on the plus button that is located in the upper right-hand corner of the screen. This will reveal a menu that allows you to scan documents, upload documents, capture photos or videos, and create new documents.

It is possible to access Word, Excel, or PowerPoint files straight from the OneDrive app, which gives it a significant amount of capability.

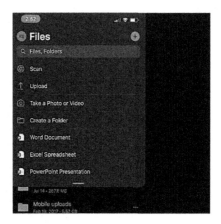

You should also keep in mind that in addition to capturing material, you can also edit pdfs right on the phone, and the OneDrive app has some fantastic features for editing pdfs. This is just one of the many things that you should keep in mind. When a PDF file is opened in the OneDrive app, there are some quite impressive annotation options available to use. If you want to put some material on the pdf, you can do that, and if you want to place a text box here, you can do that as well. If you click on the Pen icon in the upper left-hand corner of the page, what you can do now is draw on the pdf. If you simply want to write some content, you can do that. You can also correlate notes with this OneDrive file; thus, one of the amazing things is that the OneDrive app is also a very feature-rich pdf editor on your phone.

In addition to inserting text, writing something, or annotating, you can also insert shapes by clicking on the ellipses in the top right-hand corner; you can also insert a signature, images, or the date.

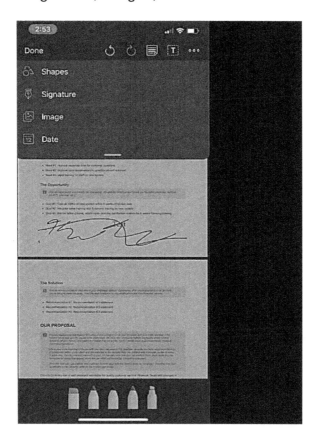

Once again, the OneDrive app gives some awesome pdf editing capabilities; and once you're done making all of your changes, you can save your pdf by clicking on **"Done"** in the top left-hand corner; this will save your pdf along with all of the edits you've made.

Working in the cloud has several advantages, one of which is that all of your files and documents are synchronized across all of your devices, making them easy to access. Additionally, you'll find some cool things you can do with your mobile device in this section.

Now that we've covered those topics, let's move on to the Office 365 account so that we can highlight a few key differences. If you look to the left, where it reads **"Shared Libraries,"** you will see that these libraries are a little bit different from one another. When you use Microsoft Teams, whenever a team is established, it appears right here, and if it's linked to OneDrive, it automatically generates a Shared folder.

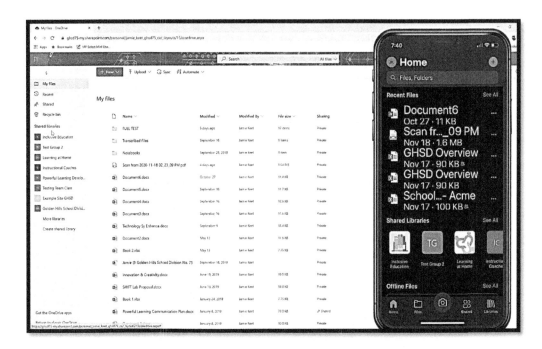

You can build a Shared Library on this page and invite other individuals to collaborate on the various papers that are required; however, anything that is stored inside Microsoft Teams will be shown on this page. When looking at the Mobile App side of it, you can see that everything is right here as well, which means that you have all of the files and you have the shared libraries on here that you can easily access.

Scanning with your Mobile App

In addition, while you are using the device, you can quickly do a **scan** by hovering your camera over a document, which you can accomplish by pressing the camera button in the center of the device. You will see that you have a variety of options, ranging from whiteboard to business card to document to photo.

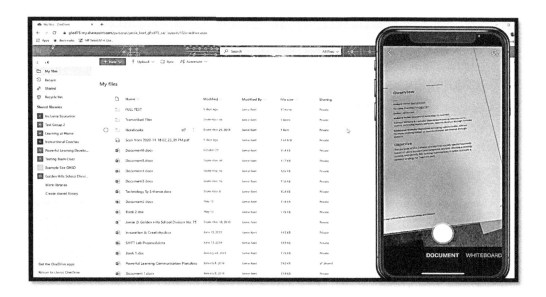

The next step is to snap the image, and after you have completed cropping it to your liking, you are going to press **"Done,"** then hit **"Done"** again, and then you are going to just hit the checkmark in the upper right-hand corner, and it will save it to your files.

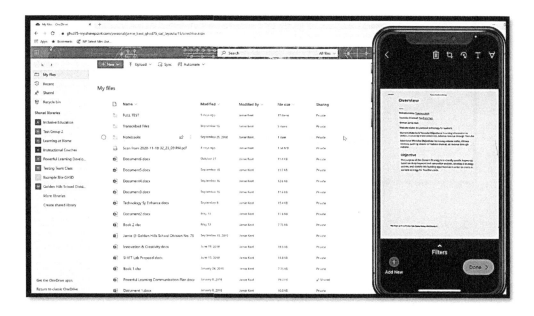

When you return to your Office 365 account and do a refresh in your OneDrive, you will be able to see the scanned picture that was completed only a few moments ago. That was simply a photo that was converted into a pdf, but what you can do is download this, and if you do that, you can open it in Microsoft Word. You will start by **opening Microsoft Word**, selecting **"Open,"** **navigating** to where you save your **downloads**, and then **opening the pdf** file that you have just downloaded. As you can see, this is a Word document. You merely snapped a photo of it on your phone, then you were able to download it from your OneDrive, and now you have opened it in Microsoft Word, where you have complete editing capabilities.

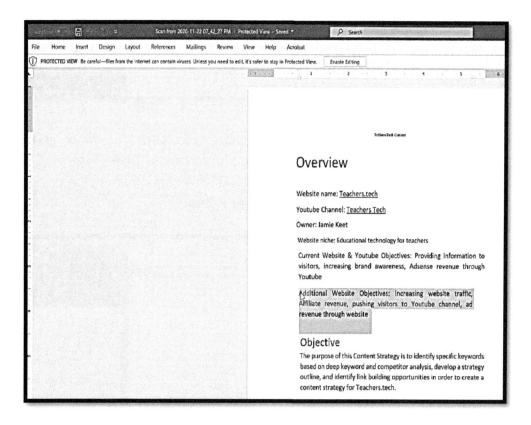

You will be able to observe, as you go, that if there is anything that needs modification, you will have the opportunity to do it here. You can scan things in, then use Microsoft Word, and then just open it up like that to quickly make some modifications to pdfs. That is a wonderful function to have, and it is something that you can do.

Exploring on your own

To gain mastery of all you have learned in this chapter, it's time to explore on your own by carrying out the following activities:

- Use your OneDrive Mobile App to create and upload images and documents to your account.
- Scan documents using the various options available and upload them.
- Upload and edit pdf files using OneDrive Mobile app.

CHAPTER 5

WHICH TOOLS FOR FILES: SHAREPOINT OR ONEDRIVE?

When it comes to using Office 365, one of the most often questions asked is, **"When should you save your files in SharePoint Online as opposed to OneDrive for Business**?" In this chapter, we are going to discuss the answer to that question. And in what kinds of circumstances do you make use of them? This is not just a topic that is asked often, but it is also an excellent one, and if you make use of Microsoft Teams, it is extremely relevant for you as well. We are going to look at each of them, discuss the similarities and differences between the two, and then explain when and why you would use either one. The emphasis here will be placed on OneDrive for Business, which is the edition of OneDrive that is included with Microsoft 365.

OneDrive and SharePoint are the two primary places in which you can save your data while using Microsoft 365. Both of these applications use the same underlying technology. If you are familiar with how to use one, you will have no trouble using the other since they are almost identical in appearance, feel, and functionality

SharePoint and OneDrive are both places where you can save files; however, why do you need two locations to keep anything in Office 365? Furthermore, how do SharePoint and OneDrive connect to Teams, which seems to be a third location where you can store your files? You should use SharePoint and OneDrive in the manner in which they were genuinely supposed to be used. The reasons for using SharePoint and OneDrive are noticeably different from one another. You want to use them both and it is not difficult at all to juggle the two; once you learn how to use them, you'll probably never go back and if you're using shared files in Outlook groups, or Microsoft Teams, you're using SharePoint Online in the background; the files tab in each app is a SharePoint document library in the background and you just happen to be accessing it and editing files through a different interface but it's still a Team site in SharePoint Online.

The Similarities

To begin, let's discuss how the two are comparable to one another. Both OneDrive and SharePoint **share the same fundamental architecture** and **set of features**; in fact, OneDrive is nothing more than a single SharePoint document library housed within a single SharePoint site that is dedicated to you alone; the only difference is that OneDrive uses a different brand name.

Both of them **support many of the same features**, such as editing Office files, Word, Excel, PowerPoint, and OneNote via Office for the web (previously known as Office online), file sizes up to 100 GB, co-authoring (simultaneous editing), version history, file sharing (both internally and externally), mobile device access, and syncing files to your computers and phones.

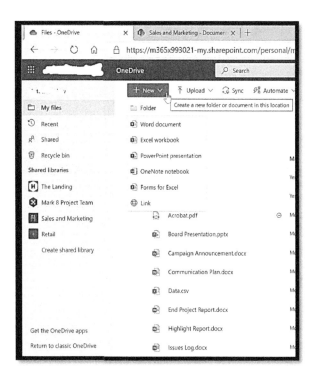

They are also both **available through Microsoft Teams**; SharePoint is the file tool that is used behind the scenes of a team or channel, while OneDrive is what is utilized when you exchange files in a private conversation inside Microsoft Teams.

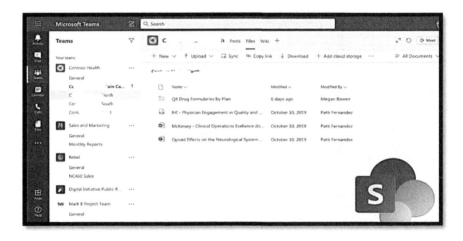

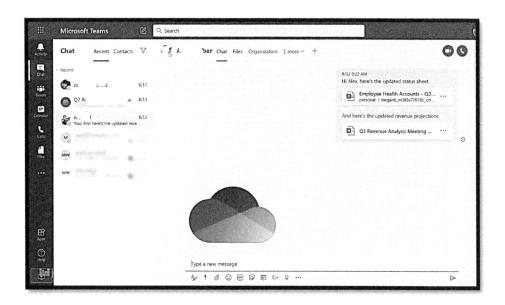

The Differences

OneDrive can be used as a **storehouse** for all of your "**Personal**" **data**. You are the only one who has access to it, so you can work on your content there. If you want to share it with other people, you can, but keeping things private is the default setting. SharePoint, on the other hand, is where you should **keep the files** associated with your **team**. Everyone on your team has access to it, and you can conduct work together in that space, which also has sharing set as its default function.

In OneDrive you can just **store documents**. It has been developed to make working on your files straightforward for you. Documents can be stored in the same manner in SharePoint as well; however, users also can **create pages** and interact with data lists, making the platform more versatile but also more difficult to use. Choose OneDrive if you are simply interested in working with documents and like things to be as straightforward as possible.

"**My Files**" is the name of the single library that OneDrive provides for the storage of your documents. In the section labeled "**My Files**," you can create new documents, upload existing ones, and organize them into folders.

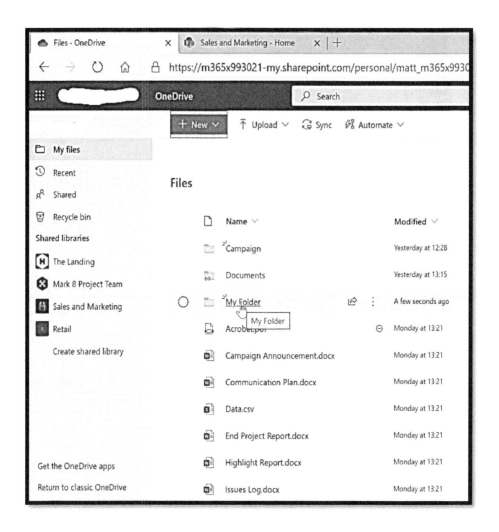

There is a default library on a SharePoint site that's named **"Documents,"** and its functionality is identical to that described above. On the other hand, a SharePoint site allows for the creation of new libraries by anybody who has access to the site, which means that you could wind up with a large number of libraries. Use SharePoint if you need the ability to store your documents in a variety of libraries, as well as the freedom to establish a large number of these libraries.

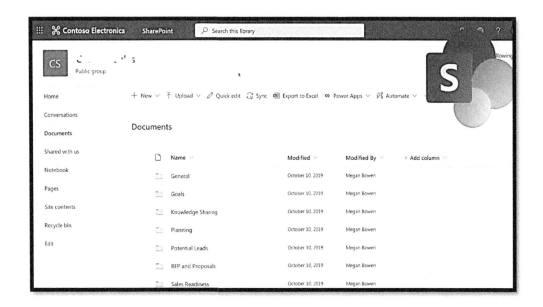

Nothing in your OneDrive is shared with anybody unless you specifically want to do so. Everything is set to be **private** until you want to share it, and it is simple to see what other people have shared and to cease sharing if you so choose. Because everything in SharePoint is **shared with the team** by default, unless you specifically tell it not to be, whatever you produce on that platform will be visible to all of your other team members. OneDrive is the location to use if you would rather work on your project in secret and then decide whether or not to share it when you are ready to do so. SharePoint is the location to keep a document if you want to share it as soon as it is generated so that other people can work on it with you, proofread it, or evaluate it.

When to Use SharePoint and OneDrive

Now that we have everything out of the way, let's discuss when to utilize OneDrive. Personal files, such as those associated with work or school, can be stored in OneDrive; however, they must be files that are unique to you. Every member of your business will have their own personal OneDrive, and the storage capacity of each OneDrive account will typically be at least 1 terabyte. OneDrive is ideal for storing two different kinds of files: first, ones that you only want for you—likely **personal files** that just shouldn't be shared; and second, **drafts of files** that you aren't ready to move into SharePoint or Teams yet for collaborative input or reviews. OneDrive is a cloud-based file storage and sync service developed by Microsoft. If you like your files to be organized in folders, you have the option to do so in OneDrive; nevertheless, how you organize your files is a matter of personal opinion. These can include notes from conferences, your health insurance and benefits files for work, your OneNote notebook for taking general notes, and a lot of draft files before you are ready to copy them to Teams to share with colleagues for input; in this case, you can keep the original copy of your files for yourself, but that decision is purely a matter of personal preference.

You can collaborate in OneDrive; however, it is particularly difficult when many individuals are working on the same files at the same time and each person is sharing separate files from their own OneDrive. When you upload files and work together on them in a centralized area like SharePoint or Teams, it makes everything a lot simpler. Additionally, when an employee leaves a business, their OneDrive is normally retired within thirty days; hence, if your team is utilizing that space to work on anything essential, you will not be delighted to discover one morning that those files have been deleted.

Therefore, OneDrive is the location for you to **save files** that are **unique** to you, **draft files** that you intend to upload to SharePoint for input evaluations, or just make them accessible to your team. Use SharePoint if you do not need any of these characteristics.

Let's go on to discussing SharePoint now. It functions best when used for two different purposes: **working on files with other people** and **publishing** them so that everyone can view them. **Team sites** are fantastic for working together on projects, and **Communication sites** are excellent for posting content.

Team websites have very **few users**, but the vast majority of them, if not all of them, have editing rights. Since you're helping them out, there's no need to limit their permissions. Team sites are to get work done; in addition, they serve as the file location behind Microsoft 365 groups, such as Outlook groups, Yammer communities, and Teams' teams. In such a scenario, every member of the group is granted automatic edit access to the content of the team site. To put it another way, SharePoint Team sites are for the things that belong to the team. **Communication sites** are typically available to practically **all members of an organization**; however, the vast majority of users are only granted read-only access to the site. In most cases, only a select few individuals are authorized to upload, edit, and remove published content. Your company's intranet will typically include Communication sites. A listing of the company's policies is an excellent illustration of this. The individuals who develop and manage such files can change the policies whenever it is required; but, the majority of visitors to the site are simply there to read the policies, and they should not have the ability to alter them as frequently as they presumably would want to be able to. Therefore, communication platforms are for the use of everyone.

The Document Circle

When it comes to juggling the two programs OneDrive and SharePoint, there is a basic set of recommendations to follow that we would refer to as "**The Document Circle**."

If you follow these instructions, you should be able to successfully manage both apps.

- You can get started on the drafting of your file in OneDrive for Business, and when you're ready, you can transfer your file to a SharePoint Team Site so that your coworkers can give feedback and evaluate it.
- You can also **compose the file** directly on the **Team site**, **save** it there, and then **call the team members** at a later time to bring them in to evaluate the file. This gives the team the most possible visibility of the document.
- When the file is finished and ready to be distributed, **publish** it to a **communication site** if it is intended for **widespread distribution**. Publish it to a **Team site** if it is something like a template for team-specific documentation or if it is for **your team** to use at a later time.

- Maintain a **functioning copy** of the document inside the **Team site** so that adjustments can be made quickly and easily while ensuring that the document remains hidden from the outside world.

Please keep in mind that the preceding is only a recommendation and not a prescription in any way shape or form. Your company can conduct things differently, but the majority of organizations utilize the concept in some form or another as a basis for their operations. Take the concept, run with it, modify it to suit your requirements, and then present it to your team so that they may perhaps debate it and figure out how you can enhance the way that you all work together.

It may seem that SharePoint, OneDrive, and their connection with Teams are complicated, however, to put it in the simplest terms possible, you will discover that you are always switching between SharePoint Communication Sites, the SharePoint Team Sites, and OneDrive. Although making things as simple as possible in Office 365 might at times result in quite hazy instructions, in this instance, The Document Circle functions rather well.

Exploring on your own

To gain mastery of all you have learned in this chapter, it's time to explore on your own by carrying out the following activities:

- Create a SharePoint account and compare it with your OneDrive account.

CHAPTER 6

ONEDRIVE FOR BUSINESS

Welcome to OneDrive for Business, and in this chapter, we will cover all that you need to know to get started with OneDrive for Business. The first step in this process will be for you to get an awareness of what OneDrive for Business is relating to cloud storage in general, how to access OneDrive for Business, how to move around it, and how to manage anything that is saved inside OneDrive. We are going to discuss how to obtain information from the recycle bin, as well as how to share information with other coworkers. To provide you with simple access to the information stored in the cloud, we will walk you through the process of syncing your OneDrive for Business account with your computer. Therefore, be ready to learn all you need to know to begin utilizing this very helpful tool for cloud storage.

What is OneDrive for Business?

OneDrive for Business is a feature that can be utilized with either the SharePoint server or Office 365. It gives you a location in the cloud where you can store, distribute, and sync the files associated with your work. You can make changes to your files and share them using any device. You can even collaborate with other people on Office documents that are being worked on at the same time using OneDrive for Business.

The concept of "**Cloud Storage**" refers to a type of cloud computing in which data is kept on a distant server and retrieved through the internet, also known as the "**cloud**." On a storage server, a cloud storage service provider is responsible for its upkeep as well as its operation and management, built on virtualization techniques for us.

Through our **subscription** to **Office 365**, Microsoft takes care of managing our OneDrive for Business accounts.

Accessing OneDrive for Business

The most straightforward method of gaining access to OneDrive for Business is to go to the website's URL, which is **portal.office.com**. This takes you to the first login screen for Office 365, and regardless of where you do your job, all you need to do is type your email address into the box given, followed by your password.

When you click the **sign-in** button, you will be sent to the Office 365 site. From there, you will be able to access all of the various components that are included in Office 365, including OneDrive for Business.

OneDrive for Business is the OneDrive that you use at work; nevertheless, you would be utilizing Office 365 at home if you had a home license for that product. After selecting **"OneDrive,"** a new tab will come up, and you will see that you have been brought to OneDrive for Business, which you will be using for the first time.

When you visit OneDrive for the first time, it provides you with some information on what this product can accomplish, which assists you in getting started with it. You indeed have a place to save files and photos, and that location is always accessible to you regardless of the device that you are using to do your task. Sharing documents and presentations is another way in which you can cooperate with OneDrive for Business. Finally, the combination of OneDrive for Business and Office results in a fantastic solution that you would like since it makes things simple to search and straightforward to modify.

Exploring OneDrive for Business

Let's go ahead and look around the site now that you've successfully logged in to your corporate OneDrive account.

The **menu** for your OneDrive for Business account is located in the upper left-hand corner of the screen. Using this, you will be able to browse the many programs that are included inside the Office 365 site. In addition, you can travel back to that site by using the button labeled "**Office 365.**" You'll note that if you choose one of the tiles, it opens up a new tab for you to go to.

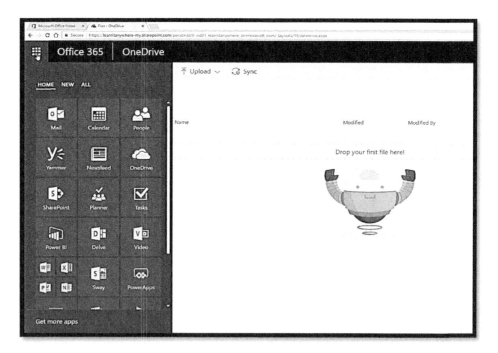

You can search for files or folders using the **search bar** that is conveniently located just below the menu and the home button on your Office 365 dashboard.

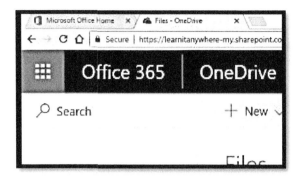

Following that, you'll see that you have the **controls** for navigating OneDrive for Business at your fingertips. You can go to your files, as well as files that you've recently made or even files that have been shared with you by other users. You also have access to a Recycle bin and a section that allows you to create new groups, although some companies ban this function entirely.

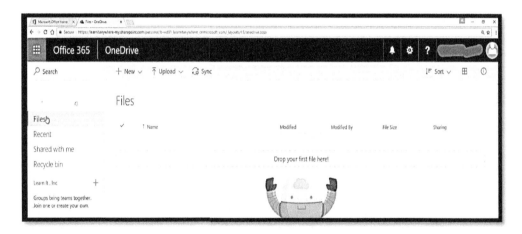

You can begin to **view** all of the various **files and folders** that you've uploaded to OneDrive for Business by navigating your way to the screen's center from wherever you are now working inside OneDrive for Business. Within OneDrive for Business, you will see that there is a row of column titles at the very top that you can utilize to **sort** or **filter** the files. You can create new files, upload existing files, and sync OneDrive with your local computer from the top menu, which is something we'll cover in more detail in a later section.

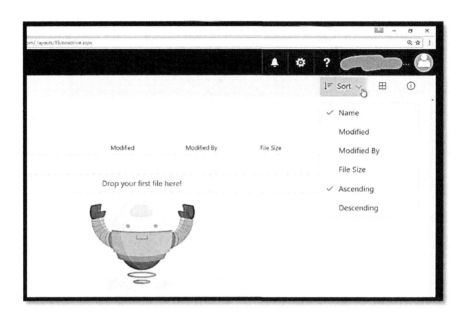

You can sort your current **view** by name in the upper right corner, and you can also alter it in the same way that you can by navigating to the individual columns inside this view. You also have the option to move between a view that is similar to a preview. In contrast to the list view, which provides you with additional information about each item, it will provide a preview of the file.

You can pull up a list of recent actions and see extra information about files that you select by using the **information panel**, which is available to you if you want to see more specifics.

You can alter the settings for OneDrive for Business or any of your other programs that are part of Office 365 by clicking on the "**Settings**" button that is located directly above the aforementioned options. In addition to the "**Help**" menu, the "**Notification**" option will let you know about any notifications that have been sent to you.

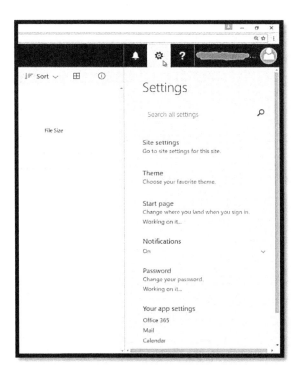

You can easily **sign out** of OneDrive for Business by selecting your name in the top right corner of the screen. This will take you to the **"About me"** section, where you can view your account and, of course, sign out, which is something you should always make sure to do if you are using a computer that is shared with other people.

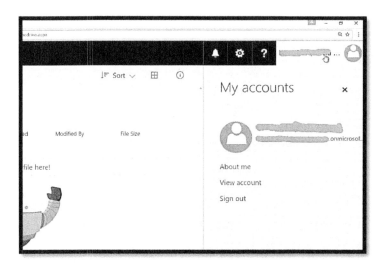

You can see that the user interface for OneDrive for Business makes use of the typical navigation on the left side of the page, that it provides you with additional options along the links at the top of the page, and that, eventually, your files and folders will begin to be added to the section in the middle of your page.

Working with Folders and Files

Let's go ahead and start creating some folders now that we've examined the user interface of OneDrive for Business; there are several methods for you to organize the information of your account, so choose one that works best for you.

If you click the **"New"** button located in the upper left corner of the screen, you will be allowed to import a variety of different file kinds. These include Links, Surveys, Notebooks, and Workbooks. Additionally, the option to create folders is available to you. After giving the folder its name, all you have to do is click the **"Create"** button, and it will immediately create a new folder and indicate that it was updated only a few moments ago.

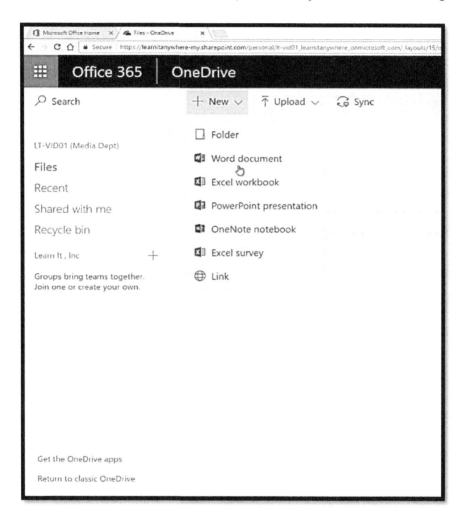

Folders that are saved locally on your computer can also be **moved** using the **drag-and-drop** method. You are going to **launch the Explorer** window, and after you have done so, you will see that you have some folders on this screen. These folders can be used to organize various pieces of information and files that are saved on your computer. If you want to take a folder from your local computer and transfer it to OneDrive for Business, you can do so by picking, dragging, and dropping this folder.

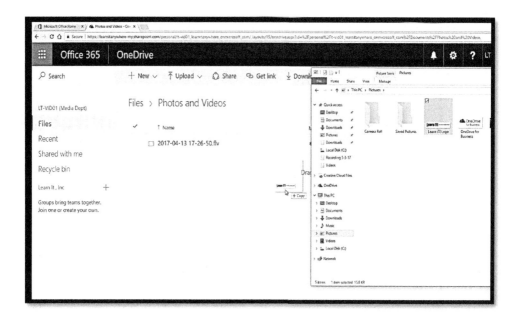

The folder, as well as any material that happens to be located inside it, will be uploaded as a result of this action. Therefore, adding folders to OneDrive for Business is as simple as clicking the **"New"** button, selecting the **"Folder"** option, and giving the folder a name.

You can also drag and drop files from any place on your local system by choosing the files, holding down the mouse button while dragging them to the screen's center, and then releasing them there. OneDrive for Business supports this functionality.

Organizing your Photos and Videos

In addition to the feature of OneDrive for Business to allow the creation of folders, you can also use it to **store media files** like pictures and videos. By clicking **"New"** and selecting **"Folder"** from the drop-down menu that appears, you can quickly create a new folder in which to save your pictures and movies.

To **access** the folder, you will just need to select it, and doing so will take you down a breadcrumb path until you reach the desired lower subfolder. It is clear to you at this point that the folder in question is vacant; nevertheless, you do own pictures and videos on your local computer

106

that you would want to include. You are now going to go to the area for videos and then just drag and drop the videos that you want to add into the folder that you have created in your OneDrive for Business account. After that, you are going to repeat the process with the photos that you have saved.

You can **import** numerous **images** at once, and to select multiple objects at once, you can use either the **Ctrl key** or the **Shift key** on your keyboard. After they have been chosen, you move them by **letting go of the mouse**, **clicking** and **holding** it, then grabbing them and dragging them to the top of the screen. You can see that it has the number of pictures that you have picked, and when you let go of the button, it uploads the images that you have chosen to the folder titled "**Photos and Videos**" in your OneDrive for Business account.

You will notice that the icon for Videos and Photos is different from one another. If you choose one of them and then open the information panel, it will provide you with information on the image that you choose, including the sort of file it is, the path to the file, and the size of the image.

Searching for files and folders

If you continue to use OneDrive for Business, the number of materials will continue to increase, making it more difficult for you to locate the specific information you want. You have access to a very strong search, but the indexing of the material may take up to a minute at times. The good thing is that you have this capability. Therefore, if you have just uploaded anything, it may not detect it instantly. However, after everything has been indexed, you will be able to search for files by using the **search** box that is located in the upper left corner of the screen. You can search for specific material inside the file, or you can use the name of the file itself.

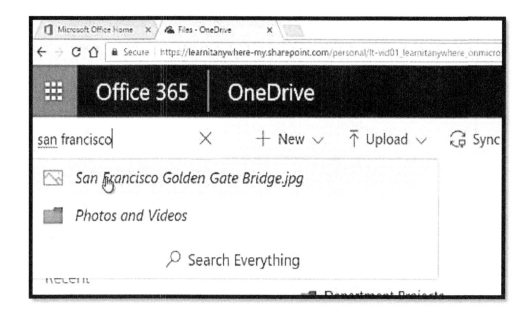

When you use the search bar to look for anything, you'll see that it not only locates the picture or document that you've saved but also locates the folder in which that item is stored. If you select the file, it will take you straight to a new tab where it will display all of the information that pertains to this file. This metadata includes the name of the file, the version of the file, and the date it was generated. If you click on the URL that is associated with that picture, you will be sent a preview of the file that you have selected.

The Search tool has a great deal of power. Again, indexing things takes a minute, so if you've just added stuff, don't panic; within a minute or two, you will be able to search for that information.

Managing Tasks Relating to Files and Folders

You'll notice that the options at the top of the screen change whenever you choose a file or folder to work with. You have access to a wider range of options, including **moving**, **copying**, **renaming**, and even **deleting** content. You do not have access to such choices while there is nothing selected.

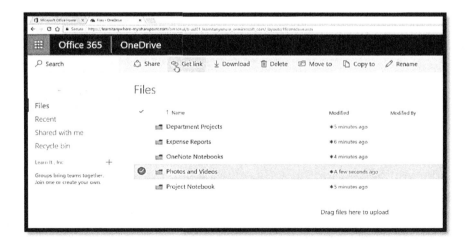

For instance, to delete data, **select** the folder or file that you want to remove, and then click the **"delete"** button on your keyboard. It will ask you to confirm that you wish to remove that item, and then you'll see in the upper right corner that it provides you with the status.

Recovering Data from the Recycle Bin

If information stored in OneDrive for Business is accidentally erased, it is possible to retrieve it from the recycling bin. In most cases, you have a period of **thirty days** to retrieve items from the recycle bin. Organizations can make adjustments to this, although it is advised that everything be recovered within thirty days.

To **restore a deleted object**, whether it be a folder or a file, just browse from the left-side menu to the **Recycle Bin**. You'll be able to view the content that was removed from this location, and all you need to do is select it. You will notice a button labeled **"Restore,"** and selecting this will cause it to be restored to its previous place, i.e., wherever it was saved when it was first created.

After you have restored a file, you will find that it is missing from your files when you return to that location. You will just need to refresh your OneDrive for Business at this point. Keep in mind that it is occasionally required to refresh the cloud-based storage; to do this, you can either use the **refresh shortcut (F5)** on your keyboard, or you can go to the top of the page and refresh your browser.

Sharing Files

Sharing is allowed with OneDrive for Business, which is one of the most significant benefits of utilizing this service. OneDrive for Business makes it simple to work together on projects; however, it is essential to become familiar with the policies that your company has established regarding sharing and collaboration, as some companies do not permit employees to share their work with individuals from other companies.

Even while you may use OneDrive to share items with big groups or departments, it is strongly recommended that you do so in a place that is more centralized, such as a SharePoint library or a shared network. This is something else that you should be aware of since it is very significant. Therefore, even if you decide to leave the business in the future for any reason, the information will still be stored on a corporate server or in a more central place.

Now that we have everything out of the way, let's look at how to share files. First things first, you should be aware that anything that you put into your OneDrive for Business is owned by you. This includes files that you have created and folders that you have uploaded. However, items that other people have shared with you are kept in a separate location. You are going to select the "**Shared with me**" option from the navigation on the left side of the screen. You will see the files that have been shared with this account in this section. This grants both your account and the account associated with this computer access to the aforementioned data, even though strictly speaking, both of these files are stored in the OneDrive of the person who shared the information with you.

If you also have a folder that has been shared with you by your colleague, that file is now stored in your colleague's OneDrive for Business account. Therefore, anytime you are searching for a file that another user has shared with you, you must browse to the **"Shared with me"** area first.

You can examine anything that was shared from, or when it was most recently edited, by using the **"Modified by"** option to sift through and categorize the results.

You can also choose an item and then utilize the icon in the upper right corner to display the information panel. This will provide you with a preview of the file, as well as show you recent activity, the original location, and other information on the file. You are free to share something with another person if it was originally shared with you and you can make changes to the file in question.

If you want to send this file to a coworker, you simply click the **"Share"** option and then just put the person's name into the text box that appears. After selecting the name, you will be prompted to provide a message. The file that was previously held by the other person who shared it with you is now considered to be shared from your account after you have clicked **"Share."** Even if you are not the file's owner, you can provide someone else access to this file due to the rights you have or the fact that this file was previously shared with you and provided you with edit privileges.

You are free to provide other people access to any files that you possess. If you have a lot of documents and you want to share one of those documents, all you have to do is choose the document you want to share, and then click **"Share"** from the menu that appears at the top.

It would not make sense to pick each item in a folder if you wanted to share everything that was included inside that folder. When you have many items chosen, even only two of them, the Share option will not be available to you. However, if you browse back via the breadcrumb trail and choose the folder that you wish to share, you will be able to share that folder. Now, anything that you add to this folder will be shared with the recipient, and if you open up the information panel on that folder, you will be able to see recent activity, the fact that it was shared, and you will be able to see that the recipient has access to these rights.

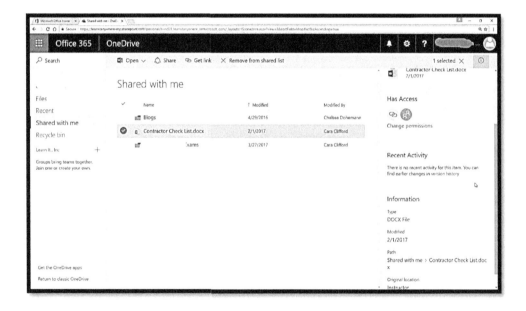

If for some reason you want to **modify those rights**, all you have to do is choose that option, and then you'll be brought to a page where you can edit the users that have access to this specific file. You will see that this person has access, and you can also remove individual rights to this, removing the privilege that you had previously granted to them. Keep in mind that because this is a web-based interface, there will be times when you will need to wait for the refresh before you can confirm that the permissions have been updated.

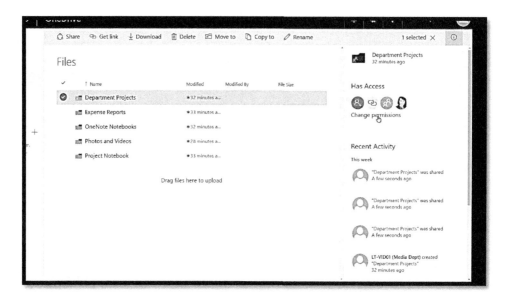

Even if file sharing is enabled inside OneDrive for business, it is important to remember to limit file sharing to a minimum and to choose just a select few individuals with whom to share files. If a whole department or the entire business has to work with a file, the best practice is to typically put it in a more centralized place. This ensures that the file or folder is not held by you, the person, but rather by the department or organization as a whole.

Using Web Apps with OneDrive for Business

You've seen in prior sections that you can immediately import folders and files into OneDrive for Business using the drag-and-drop method, but you can also create new ones here. You have seen how easy it is to create folders by just choosing the **"New Folder"** option and naming the file. However, in addition to folders, you can also create Word documents, Excel spreadsheets and workbooks, PowerPoint presentations, OneNote notebooks, Excel surveys, and even Links.

If you select the Word Document, you'll see that rather than starting Microsoft Word on your local system, you're still working inside the online browser. This is because when you select the Word Document, the web browser loads the document itself. This is the Word web app, often known as Word Online, which is a thin client that you can access via your browser.

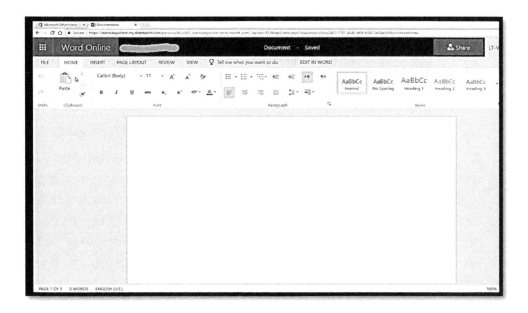

The advantage of using this tool is that even if you do not have Microsoft Office installed on your local computer or if you have an older version that is no longer supported, you are still able to utilize this online version on any device. You'll note that the interface you get here is somewhat similar to that of Word 2010 and later versions. As a component of the Ribbon interface, this consists of the command tabs that run across the top of the window. You have the File tab, which provides you with the ability to save or share, create new documents or access the information; your Home tab, which provides you with all of the common formatting options and styles; the Insert tab, which allows you to insert things such as tables or pictures, links, or comments; and the Page Layout tab, which allows you to change the orientation or size of your paragraph or adjust the spacing between sentences. You'll note that there are fewer options available to you on the View tab as well as the Review page when compared to the ones you have in the local client.

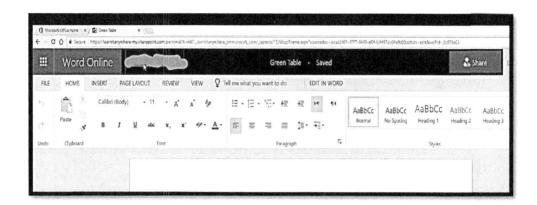

You are unable to make a mail merge or track changes while using the online edition of Word; but, the vast majority of the functions that are accessible to you when using the desktop program are included in the web-based version (the web app). You can take this document and change it in Word at any point in time, and you will have access to that choice here. When you click **"Edit in Word,"** it will open Office 2016, bring up the Word program, and ask you to sign in to your account. If you have already signed in, it will skip this step.

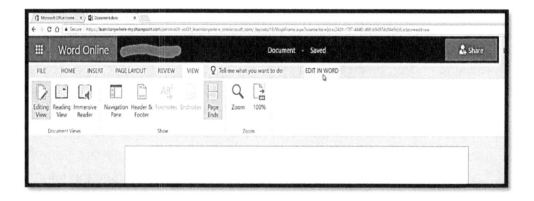

After you have enabled editing, you will be able to edit the document using the full capabilities of Word 2016, or whatever version of Word you have installed on your computer. You'll notice that there is a refresh symbol around the **"Save"** button in the upper left corner of the screen. This is a confirmation that the file will be saved to your OneDrive for Business account.

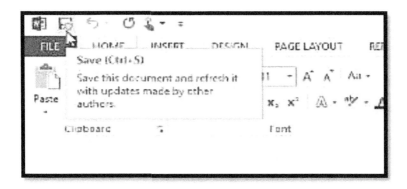

After you have finished adding your information, inserting your table, and formatting it using one of the available formatting tools, you will be brought back to Word online, where you can refresh the page to see the newly added information. Bear in mind that there may be occasions when you will need to refresh it before it will reveal the information contained inside your document.

When using the online versions of the programs, one of the extremely helpful things is the fact that you can change the file name by clicking on the file name at the top of the page. This is one of the things that makes working inside the online versions of the applications easy. It saves automatically because you are working inside a web application; hence, it is saving automatically and displaying the saved symbol to you.

If you want to go back to your library, all you have to do is choose your name, which in this instance refers to the method by which you're signed into this device. This takes you back to OneDrive, where you'll find the Word document that you just saved. You get access to online apps for Excel, PowerPoint, and OneNote in addition to the web app for Microsoft Word. OneNote is an application that can be used to create notebooks, and when you select a **OneNote notebook**, the program prompts you to give the Notebook a name before directing you to click the "**Create**" button.

OneNote, much like Microsoft Word, is available both as an online program and as a local application that can be found on your computer. The Web App will use the user interface of the browser that you are now working in. The name of the Note-Book is shown just above the waffle that can be found in the upper left-hand corner, and there is also a means to go back to the OneDrive for Business library.

You can enter tags in addition to the sections and pages that make up a notebook, which can assist you in remembering information that is important to you.

The capability to **create Surveys** is quickly becoming one of the most popular tools available within OneDrive. Excel surveys enable you to not only construct a form but also save the results of the survey within Excel, allowing you to analyze the gathered information. To do this, you will get started by making a brand-new Survey. When you start the process of creating a survey, it will first produce an Excel file.

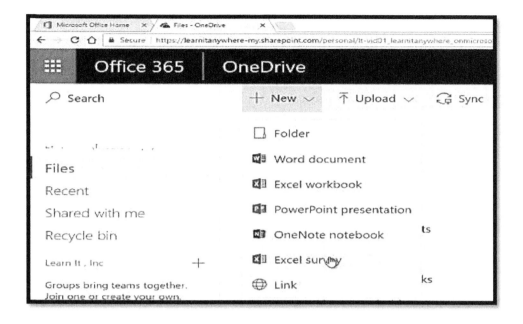

The Excel spreadsheet is visible in the background, but when you click the button, it brings up the **"Edit survey"** window in the foreground. From this window, you can give the survey a title. After that, you are going to put in the first question that you have. You will be able to pick a subtitle for that question, choose the sort of answer that will be required (a paragraph of text, numbers, dates, and times in addition to choices), and you will require that this question have information.

To add a new question, just select **"Choice"** from the answer type drop-down menu that appears after clicking on the **"Add New Question"** button. After you have entered all of your selections, you have the option to stipulate that the column must include certain information. It is also advised that the other option be used, providing individuals with the opportunity to choose more alternatives.

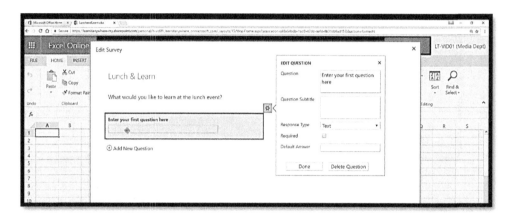

Once you are done adding your questions, you can save and see the survey. When it saves it, you will be able to see what it is going to look like to your users when they fill it out. First, they will enter their names, and then they will choose what they would be the most interested in as their answer.

A URL is generated for you to use when you want to share the survey. You simply need to send out the URL by email, and people will be routed straight to the form rather than to the Excel spreadsheet. When people begin filling out the form that you've supplied, the survey, you'll receive new rows for each answer laid out in the shape of a table as they come in.

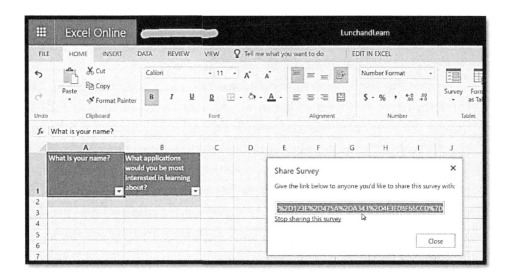

After you have closed out this window, you will see that there is a button labeled "**Survey**" on the Home tab of the Ribbon. After you have created the survey, you can come here to **view** the survey, **edit** the survey, **delete** the survey, or **share** the **survey** with other people.

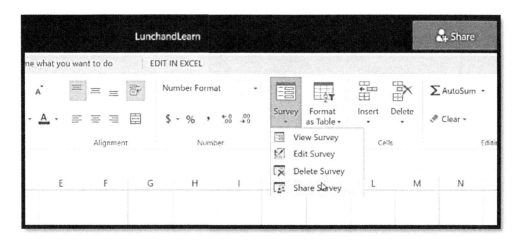

Again, when you are finished making changes to your survey and are ready to return to OneDrive for business, all you have to do is select your name in the upper-left corner of the screen. This will bring you back to the files section of OneDrive for business, where you will be able to view all of the different files that you have created in addition to the survey.

Synchronizing With Your Personal Computer

Since OneDrive for Business is hosted in the cloud, the only way to access it is via the Office 365 interface, which you are already familiar with from the beginning of this guide. You can, however, **sync OneDrive for Business with your local computer**, and you'll find that doing so makes dealing with files stored in OneDrive much simpler and more comfortable. This option is available to you via the OneDrive for Business website. Creating a path from your local workstation to these files in the cloud is practically all that is involved here. You should only do this on a computer that can be accessed by you and is allowed by your company. You shouldn't sync work data to a personal machine unless your firm allows you to do so.

You are going to go ahead and choose the **"Sync"** option from the links located at the very top.

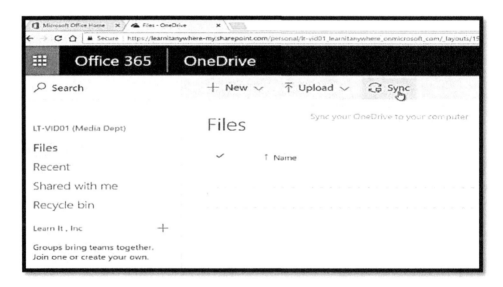

It requires you to **sign in**, and you need to check that it is using the **login details** for your OneDrive for **Business account**, including your username and your employer's email address.

After that, you can choose "**Next**" to continue going through the various pieces of information, and it will show you all of the various folders that need to be synchronized, even files that are not presently located in a folder. You have the option of deselecting any of these options if there are any files that you would prefer not to have synchronized, such as older files or things that you would prefer not to have taking up space on your device. If this is not the case, you will proceed to say, "**Sync all files and folders in OneDrive**," and you will see that it is using the name of your organization to indicate that it is your OneDrive for Business.

123

123

You should now be able to see that the "**OneDrive for Business**" folder that you established is shown in your computer's File Explorer, and you should also notice that you have copies of the files that you generated in OneDrive for Business.

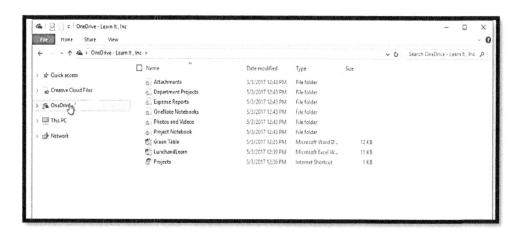

Take caution since some PCs have more than one OneDrive installed. The vast majority of Windows 10 machines will have a personal OneDrive as part of the basic package; however, you will need to check that you are seeing the OneDrive associated with your employer. You won't have to worry about completing this stage since several organizations will do it for you.

Uploading files to OneDrive for Business via the File Explorer

If you want to add a file to this library here, all you have to do is select any local application, such as Word, Excel, or PowerPoint, open up your new workbook, and then when you choose "**File**," "**Save as**," you can navigate to the **OneDrive** through your company name. To restate, this is the **business version of OneDrive online**. The first OneDrive in this scenario would be a "personal" OneDrive; thus, you must make use of the OneDrive that displays your corporate name.

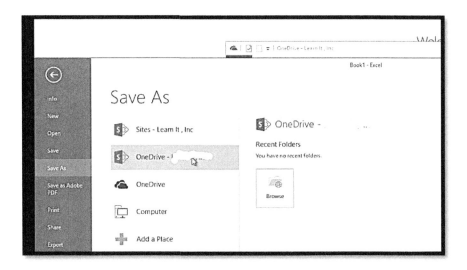

You can now give this document a **name**, **save** it, and **exit** the File.

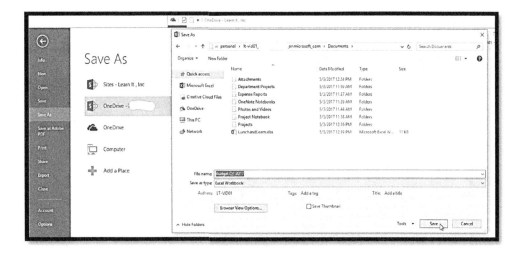

Now, when you **refresh** via your Explorer window, you'll notice that the document has been saved, and if you navigate back to OneDrive Online and refresh your screen, you'll find that the document has been saved instantaneously. Dealing with OneDrive for Business becomes just as easy and simple as working with any other local disk, network drive, or even storing items on your desktop thanks to this feature. Therefore, rather than taking the risk of something important being lost if your computer contracts a virus or is stolen, you can relax in the knowledge that you can access the files stored in your OneDrive for Business account from any location, on any device, so long as you have the email address and password associated with your employer.

Collaborating with Web Apps

The final benefit of using OneDrive for Business is that it has a function that allows for simultaneous collaboration. If you have a document that you have shared with others, then we will discuss the several ways in which you can access this document and make changes at the same time as another person.

You are going to begin by navigating to the location of your document. When you initially choose the document, it will take you to a view-only mode where you will have the option to either edit the workbook in the local application or the Web App; you are going to select the latter option to be able to edit the workbook in the browser.

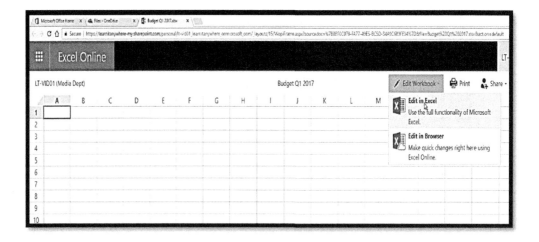

When you do this, in the upper right corner of the screen, you will instantly be able to see whether another person is also editing the document, and you will also be able to see where that other person is typing. You will see the active cell of the person who is adding information, and if you go into that cell and start entering information, someone else will see what you have typed.

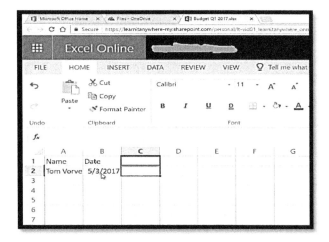

Using the Skype for Business platform

You can talk with other individuals who are now editing the file in the upper right corner of the screen. When you pick that, it will activate the **Skype for Business** Web interface, where you will be able to communicate with anybody else who is presently working with the file.

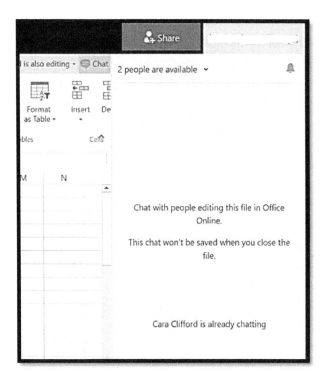

When it comes to being able to update material while another person is also altering it, this kind of cooperation is quite useful since it allows you to do both at the same time. Having said that, it is not the kind of thing that should be done with documents that have privacy rules and that need to be tracked with the modifications that are made. It is important to keep in mind that if a file is saved in OneDrive for Business, shared with you, or if you have shared it with someone else, then more than one person may be editing the file simultaneously inside the program. You should keep in mind that saving will be done automatically; thus, all you need to do is navigate back to your OneDrive for Business library. Once you are there, you will be able to check who was the most recent person to alter this document.

Exploring on your own

To gain mastery of all you have learned in this chapter, it's time to explore on your own by carrying out the following activities:

- Create a OneDrive for Business Account.
- Explore the features and get familiar with the interface.
- Create and upload files and folders and sync these across your devices.
- Using other Microsoft Online apps, create and share files with your colleagues.
- Explore the Skype platform while collaborating with your colleague.

CHAPTER 7

MICROSOFT ONEDRIVE TOP TIPS AND TRICKS

This chapter will review everything that you've learned up to this point, and then we'll go on to demonstrate the top 10 useful tips and tricks for using Microsoft OneDrive.

The Summary of it all

Let's do a quick review of everything you've picked up so far before we go on to the next step. It has been established that OneDrive is a cloud storage provider. It's the same thing as if you've used Google Drive or iCloud from Apple in the past; the only difference is that this is Microsoft's version of the service. In essence, you are storing your data on servers managed by Microsoft; however, why on earth would you ever want to do that?

To be specific, there are three primary advantages:

To begin, you have access to all of your files no matter where you are. This means that if you were to go on a tour, you would still be able to access all of your data even though you would be away from home. You can also make backups of your information and secure them; for example, even if your laptop is submerged in a pot of chocolate that is simmering, your contents will not be lost. You also can share and collaborate on your files. For example, if you and your team are working on a project, you can share the project with them, and everyone in the team can work on the same recipe at the same time.

You will need to subscribe to OneDrive's Premium plan if you want to make the most of the features it offers. If you subscribe to the Microsoft 365 family plan, you can purchase it for a one-time payment of one hundred dollars and receive 6 terabytes of total storage space as well as a host of additional applications, including Microsoft Outlook, Word, Excel, and PowerPoint, in addition to all of that storage space.

Now that we've gotten that out of the way, let's move on to some useful tips and tricks that will make your time spent using OneDrive more effective.

Uploading from Your Phone's Camera

Regardless of whether you have an iPhone or an Android phone, you can use OneDrive to back up all of the photos and videos that are stored on your phone. To begin, you will need the OneDrive software, which can be downloaded from the **App Store** on an iPhone or the **Play Store** on an android phone. This is a must for being able to back up your images and videos that are stored on your phone. You only need to search for **"OneDrive,"** and the OneDrive app should come up as the first result. If you do not already have it, go ahead and install it; otherwise, click the **"Open"** button. When you have finished downloading and installing the OneDrive app on your phone, you will be very close to being able to upload all of the images that are currently stored on your phone to OneDrive. Make sure that this is activated by clicking on your profile image, which is located in the upper left-hand corner of the screen. This will bring up a menu.

Next, choose **"Settings"** from the menu.

To upload photos and files from your camera, go to the "**Settings**" menu and scroll approximately halfway down to the section labeled "**Files and Photos**."

You can select which of your online accounts you want images to be uploaded to inside the "**Camera Upload**" section. Make sure that your primary account is being checked. You have a couple of different options available to you down below: you can indicate whether you want to use a mobile network, and you can have that toggled off. This is especially helpful if you don't want to use it up for backup; instead, you'll wait until you have wi-fi before you back up your photos. You can also choose whether or not you want to add videos. Since videos need a much larger amount of storage space, you have the option of deciding whether or not you want all of that information to be stored in your OneDrive account. In this scenario, you need to make sure that this is toggled on if you want to back up both your images and your videos. Just below it, you'll find a section where you can organize your photos. If you, have it set to a month, it will organize all of your images according to the month in which they were taken? You can also set it to the year, or you could just have it all go to a pictures folder with no categorization at all in place.

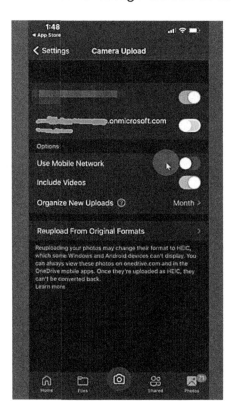

After you have finished setting these, you will see some information inside OneDrive that informs you that your pictures are in the process of uploading. You'll also see a symbol in the bottom right corner of the screen letting you know that this picture is only available on your phone at the moment; after it's been synchronized to your OneDrive, you won't be able to see this icon anymore.

Scan Documents

This takes us to the second tip, which is that you can scan documents using the OneDrive app, which is powered by technology developed by **Office Lens**. Office Lens is capable of doing a job that is far better than what the default camera on your phone can achieve. To make use of this feature inside the OneDrive app, choose the **camera icon** located at the very bottom of the screen. This activates your camera, and once it's open, you can use it to scan your phone for a picture or document.

You can take photos also of whiteboards, business cards, and regular photos in addition to being able to take photos of documents. If you are modifying a document, choose **"Document"** from the options. You will see that the edges of the document are highlighted in a blue box, and if that successfully catches your document, you will be able to snap a picture of it.

You will click the **"Confirm"** button after it has now taken a snapshot of the document and determined where the edges are located. Your document is now ready for you to see, and it has undergone significant editing. You have some options below that allow you to add other photos to the scan, apply various filters to it, crop it, and then you have some more options if you want to rotate it or maybe add some text to it. If you are okay with the information that you have at this location, click the **"Done"** button.

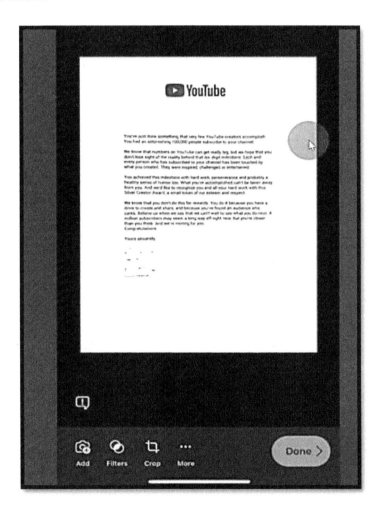

The next screen will provide you the opportunity to choose a destination for saving this file. You just place it inside the folder labeled **"Files,"** and after you are all prepared, you will choose the check mark from the menu.

You can now see the document that you scanned in on your personal computer, and you can attest to the fact that this is a pretty nice document scan; the background looks really good, and it captured all of the detail, and all you had to do to get it was taking a photo of it with your phone, and it is now available on your personal computer as well as anywhere else that you happen to be working.

Share, as well as work together

This brings us to the next tip, which is that you can share files stored in the cloud and work together with other people on those files. Let's imagine you're on **onedrive.com** and can see a whole number of files that you want to share with some of the other members of your team so that you can all collaborate on the same file at the same time. You only need to right-click on the file, and there will be an option to **share** it in the context menu that appears.

If you click on that, the shared dialog will pop up, and you will see right at the top of the window that the document can be edited by anybody who you share it with. You can modify that setting simply by clicking on that option, especially if you just want a certain person to be able to access it. You will enter in the names of the individuals you wish to share it with right down here, and you also have the option of typing in a message for them. Now, if you don't want to fill in any names up here, you also have the option of simply **copying a link** to this file by clicking on that option. This will set a link on the clipboard, and you can then paste it into an email or anyplace else that you want to share it with someone else. When you are ready to share, you will need to choose the option that says **"Send"** from the menu.

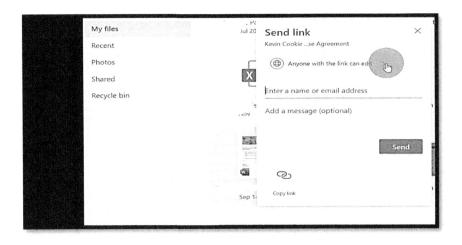

Files can be shared directly via Windows, in addition to being able to do so through the website onedrive.com. You will find the same document on your computer by using **File Explorer** to access it. You can right-click on it, and right here at the top, you'll see all of the various controls for OneDrive. If you choose to share the file, a shared dialog box will appear on the screen that is very identical to the one you saw on onedrive.com.

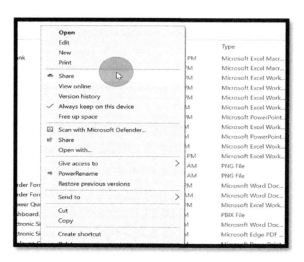

To share this file with others, you can either copy the link, or fill in the names of the people you want to share it with, and simply write a message.

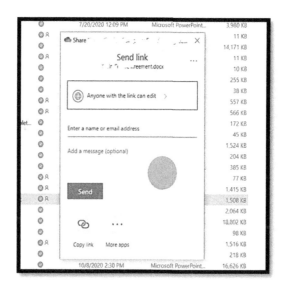

When you share anything with others, whether documents, photos, or anything else, you all have the opportunity to collaborate on it. When you make changes to the information shown on your screen, your coworker will almost immediately see those alterations reflected on their screen. Because of this, working together is very simplified.

This brings us to tips number four and five, both of which pertain to the concept of sharing in some way.

You had been sharing a single file up until this point. Nevertheless, you may also share a complete folder with other people. You may right-click on it here, just as you would with a file, and then choose the **"Share"** option from the menu that appears.

This sets up the shared dialog once again, with the exception that this time you click on the text that states **"Anyone with this link can edit."**

Share link Expiration

This takes us to the fourth tip about sharing, which is that you can make the links that you share expire after a certain amount of time. At the very bottom of the link settings section is where you'll find the option to **choose an expiry date**. If you don't want to keep sharing something forever because you can't predict what others are going to be interested in a year from now, then this is helpful. You will now choose this option and choose a date for it to become invalid after using it.

When you click on this, you will be able to share the link with another person, but they will only have a very small time in which they can view the contents of any folder you have in this place.

Share Link That Requires a Password to Access

Just beneath that, you'll find our fifth tip, which is that you can **protect** the shared links you create with a **password**. Therefore, a password must be entered into this box here.

Once you're all ready to go, including deciding on the expiry date and creating a password, click the **"Apply"** button.

Now that you've applied those various changes, you will see a calendar icon informing you that it is about to expire, and you will also see an icon indicating that it is locked, and now you can proceed to share this file exactly as you did before.

The Personal Vault

This brings us to the sixth tip, which is to create a Personal Vault. It is the one on your OneDrive account that resembles a safe of some kind. What exactly is it, and how does it vary from a regular folder in OneDrive's interface? If you click on any of these folders, you will be able to access their contents; however, you are not able to do this with the Personal Vault. After clicking on it, you'll need to utilize something called two-factor authentication to prove your identity. You are going to pull out your phone, enter the secret code, and when it has confirmed your identity, it is going to log you into the Personal Vault.

A Personal Vault is an excellent place for storing important documents and photos, such as copies of your passport and driver's license.

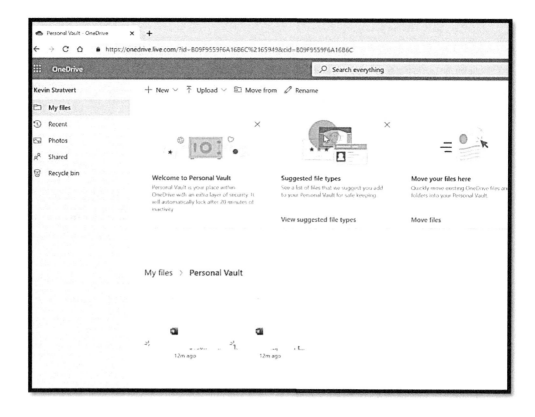

When you are through reviewing all of the data stored in your "Personal Vault", you can log out of the service by clicking on the icon located in the upper right-hand corner of the screen, as seen in the following image.

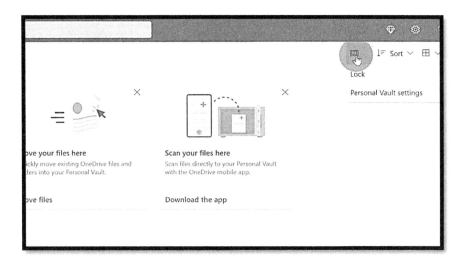

This will send you back to the main view of your OneDrive account, and your "Personal Vault" or Safe will still be locked. If you do not log out of the vault within 20 minutes, it will do so automatically and you will be required to employ two-factor authentication to regain access to your vault beyond that point.

Version History

This brings us to the seventh tip, which is that you can see the version history of any document that you keep on OneDrive, whether it be a Word document, an Excel spreadsheet, or a PowerPoint Presentation. You can revert to a version that existed before the changes that were made if you or another user makes modifications to the site and decides that you do not like the results of those modifications.

Simply log into OneDrive and navigate to the file you want to see the history of. You can use the context menu that appears when you right-click on it to get the "**Version History**" option. This option is located at the very bottom of the menu.

When you do so, the Version History viewer will come up, and you will be able to locate the most recent version of this document on the left-hand side of the window that appears.

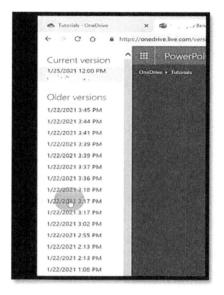

You can also view all of the older versions of the document right here. If you want to return to an earlier version, all you have to do is click on the text that describes the version you want to return to, and you will be transported back in time to that earlier version. You can then resume your work from the point where you left off.

Save your documents to your device or OneDrive

The eighth tip is that you have the option of **keeping your files** just on **OneDrive** or both on **OneDrive and your computer**. If you have File Explorer open and are currently working inside OneDrive, you can right-click on any of your files by navigating to the section containing them. Right here in this context menu, you'll see all of the various OneDrive settings, and you can choose whether or not you want to "**Always keep on this device**." This indicates that the file will be stored on both your local computer as well as on OneDrive.

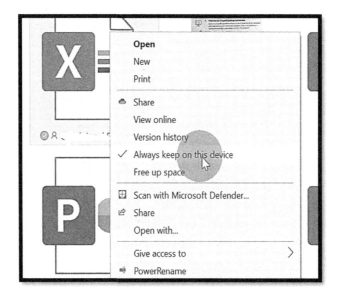

If you wish to keep it exclusively on OneDrive and save up some space on your computer, you can select the "**Free up space**" option from the menu.

For all of your data, you will want to decide to always keep on this device if you are a huge fan of making multiple backups and want to have things backed up on OneDrive as well as on your computer.

Embed Files on Your Websites

You can embed files from your OneDrive account into web pages, which brings us to our ninth tip. For instance, you have a document that you want to share with others and you want to upload it to the website of your firm so that they can do so. Right-clicking on the document will bring up the "**Embed**" option which can be found inside this menu's options, and clicking on the ellipsis will provide all of the available options (Within this menu there's the option to "Embed").

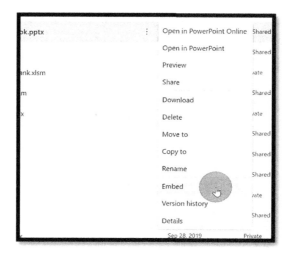

If you click on that option, a menu will appear on the right-hand side of the page. In this menu, you will find the **embed code**. After clicking on this, you'll want to choose "**Copy**" and once you've done so, you'll have the embed code ready to paste into your website.

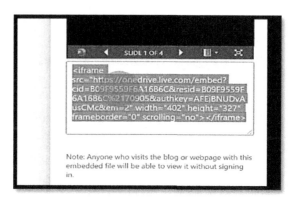

To embed content on Google Sites, go to the right-hand side of the page, click the **"Insert"** tab, and then choose the **"Embed"** option from the menu that appears.

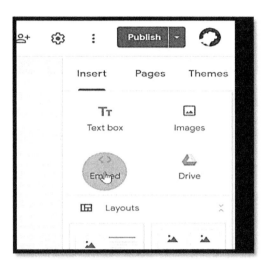

This will open a new dialogue in which you will have the option to either **embed code** or a **link**. Since you have already copied an Embed code, you will need to click on that option and then paste the code that you copied from OneDrive.

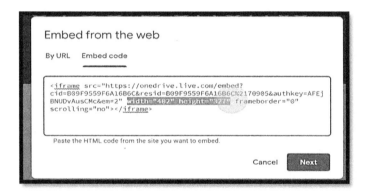

You have the option of **adjusting the width and the height** right here inside the code if you want your content to look bigger; otherwise, you can leave it at the default setting and then click on the "**Next**" button. This is an intriguing feature.

You will be able to get a preview of what it is that you are going to embed in this section. If it seems to be exactly as you would want it to, click the **"Insert"** button.

You have now successfully put your document into your page. If you want it to seem bigger, you can go in and change the width and height, then click on the **"Publish"** button.

Restore your OneDrive

This is the last tip, and it's a good one: if you have files that you mistakenly erased or if anything awful occurs and you lose everything in your OneDrive account, don't despair because you can restore everything in your OneDrive account.

First things first, let's have a look at the several ways you can **retrieve specific files**. Over on the left-hand side, there's the Recycle bin. When you click on this, you will be presented with a list of all of the files that you have deleted recently; you can go through this list, and you will be able to restore individual files. You also have the option of restoring everything that is currently in your recycle bin. Because items are only kept in the recycling bin for 30 days, if you delete anything and realize that you need it again, the sooner you act, the better.

Now, let's imagine that something very terrible occurred, and you need to restore everything that was stored in your OneDrive. You can do that as well, and you don't have to do it via the recycle bin; instead, go up to the upper right-hand corner where there's a **Settings** gear. After clicking on this, go to the next step and choose "**Options.**"

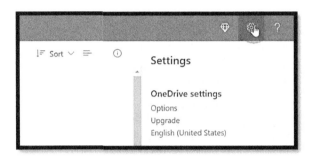

You can **restore your OneDrive** to an earlier version by going into the OneDrive options and selecting "**Restore your OneDrive**" from the list of options on the left-hand side of the screen. You can restore it to any point in time up to one month ago. You have the option to restore data from yesterday, seven days ago, three weeks ago, or even a date and **time of your choice by using the drop-down menu:**

If you choose any one of these options, you will not only be able to see when changes are made to your OneDrive account, but you will also be able to see what those changes were. Once you're ready to restore all of your files, you can click on the button that says "**Restore**".

This is very similar to the Version History that we looked at before for an individual document; however, this applies to your whole OneDrive account rather than just that one document. It's a very useful feature for ensuring that you never lose important stuff, so make sure you use it.

Exploring on your own

Now that you are acquainted with OneDrive, make it a point to use the helpful hints that you have discovered in this chapter to good use while you are working with your OneDrive to achieve greater mastery of OneDrive, save time, and become more productive with OneDrive.

INDEX

Y

Yahoo, 40

Printed in Great Britain
by Amazon

39487974R00086